Scotland's leading educational publishers

Practice Papers for SQA Exams

CfE Higher

History

Practice Papers

D0244085

ISBN 9780007590957

Published by
Leckie & Leckie Ltd
An imprint of HarperCollins*Publishers*
Westerhill Road, Bishopbriggs, Glasgow, G64 2QT
T: 0844 576 8126   F: 0844 576 8131
leckieandleckie@harpercollins.co.uk   www.leckieandleckie.co.uk

Publisher: Katherine Wilkinson
Project Managers: Craig Balfour and Keren McGill

Special thanks to
Ink Tank (cover design)
QBS (layout)
Louise Robb (copy edit and proofread)
Donna Cole (proofread)

A CIP Catalogue record for this book is available from the British Library.

Printed in Italy by Grafica Veneta S.p.A.

Acknowledgements

Part A: The Wars of Independence, 1249–1328

Source C adapted from *Robert the Bruce: King of Scots* by Ronald McNair Scott. Reproduced courtesy of Nigel McNair Scott DL.

Source D adapted from *The Kings and Queens of Scotland* by Richard Oram. Reproduced courtesy of The History Press.

Part C: The Treaty of Union, 1689–1740

Source A adapted from Keith Brown, *Kingdom or Province?: Scotland and the Regal Union, 1603-1715*, 1992, Palgrave Macmillan. Reproduced with permission of Palgrave Macmillan.

Part D: Migration and Empire, 1830–1939

Source B adapted from *New Arrivals* by Tony Jaconelli, published on the 'Our Glasgow Story' website: http://www.ourglasgowstory. com/story.php?sid=98.

Source D adapted from *Success in the 'Lucky' Country* by Ian Donnachie, taken from *That Land of Exiles: Scots in Australia* (1988), crown copyright.

Part E: The Impact of the Great War, 1914–1928

Source B adapted from *The Scottish Economy and the First World War* by Clive H. Lee. Reproduced courtesy of Birlinn.

Source C adapted from *Scottish Popular Politics: From Radicalism to Labour* by W. Hamish Fraser. Reproduced courtesy of Birlinn.

Source D adapted from *The Scottish Nation: 1700–2007* (2006) by T.M. Devine. Reproduced by permission of Penguin Books Ltd.

Whilst every effort has been made to trace the copyright holders, in cases where this has been unsuccessful, or if any have inadvertently been overlooked, the Publishers would gladly receive any information enabling them to rectify any error or omission at the first opportunity.

Introduction

The Higher History course has changed: there is now only a single exam, to be completed in 2 hours and 20 minutes. This book is going to prepare you for that exam and give you advice, guidance and practice papers to help you gain the mark you deserve. It will also show you how the source-based questions differ and how the essay structure and approach has slightly changed.

There are always three topics covered in the Higher History course. The Scottish topic is examined in source-based questions and you should aim to complete this part in 1 hour. The British and European and World topics are examined by one essay per topic and you should aim to complete each of these in 40 minutes.

TOP TIP
One exam = 2 hours and 20 minutes, broken down as:
- 1 hour for three source-based questions
- 40 minutes for one British essay
- 40 minutes for one European and World essay

Higher History source-based questions – Scottish topic

You will study a Scottish topic, which will be used to complete three source-based questions:

- One 'Evaluate the usefulness' question

- One 'How Fully?' question and

- One 'Compare the views' question

The 'Evaluate the usefulness' question

This is worth 6 marks in the final exam and asks you to establish how useful a primary source is in relation to a historical event that you have studied in your Scottish topic.

When answering this question at Higher level you need to always consider the following:

- The origin and possible purpose of the source

- The content of the source

- Your own knowledge

The origin and possible purpose of the source

Author – who produced the source?

Ask yourself the following questions:

- Is the author an eyewitness to the event in question? (Remember to say what the event is.)
- Could they be showing an element of bias?
- Is the source only showing one person's view of the event?
- Could they be writing it for some form of financial gain?
- Could they be exaggerating to make it more sensational?
- Is the author an expert on the event in question? (Remember to say what the event is.)
- Using the advantage of hindsight will the author be neutral/balanced in their viewpoint?
- Will the author have researched the topic well?

> ### TOP TIP
> Make a judgement on the author and state whether that makes the source more or less useful, for 1 mark.

Purpose – why is the source being written?

Consider the following:

- If the source is an extract from a newspaper, it could contain bias and exaggeration.
- If the source is from a personal memoir it is more likely to be the documentation of the event and therefore unbiased.
- If the source is an extract from a politician's speech it could show an element of bias.
- If the source is a piece of propaganda it may be biased.

> ### TOP TIP
> Make a judgement on the purpose of the source and whether that makes it more or less useful, for 1 mark.

Timing – when was the source written?

Ask yourself the following questions:

- Was it written at the time in question? (You must state exactly what the event in question is.)
- Why would it be useful to have a source from the time of the event in question?
- Was it written a long time after the event?
- Why would it be better to have a source from years after the event happened with the benefit of hindsight?

> ### TOP TIP
> Make a judgement on the date of the source and whether it makes the source more or less useful, for 1 mark.

Type of source – what is the source and does that affect its usefulness?

Different types of source:

- Speech – would this be bias?
- Diary – would a personal account give an honest viewpoint (but only one)?
- Government document – would this have to be factual and unbiased?
- Newspaper article – would this show bias and possible exaggeration?

> ### TOP TIP
> Make a comment on the type of source and how this could affect its usefulness, for 1 mark.

The content of the source

What does the source say and how does that help you to answer the question?

- What has helped you identify that the source is or isn't useful?
- What information from the source has helped you answer the question and state whether the source is useful or not?
- What information from the source tells you more about what the question is asking?

Give two valid points from the source.

> ### TOP TIP
> Take two points from the source content to gain 2 marks.

Your own knowledge

What omissions are there? (What crucial information about the event is being left out?)

- Does the source only give you one viewpoint and limit the amount of information on the event in question?
- Is the source telling the whole story or only selecting certain information about the event in question?

Ensure you give two knowledge points that are missing from the source.

> ### TOP TIP
> When identifying evidence and facts that are missing from the source, ensure that you provide two points to gain full marks.

The 'How fully' question

This is worth 9 marks in the final exam and allows you to identify relevant information from the source given, as well as provide relevant recalled knowledge to describe and explain the question/issue being highlighted within the Scottish topic you have studied.

When answering this question at Higher level you need to always consider the following:

- Your opening statement should make it clear how fully the source describes or explains the issue at the centre of the question. Generally, you can state that the source describes/ explains the issue to an extent. To what extent is up to your judgement; without it you can only receive 2 out of the 9 marks available.

- You should then go on to find three points from the source that help answer the question.

- The final stage is to provide up to seven points that are not present in the source from your recalled knowledge on the issue.

TOP TIP
This question relies upon a good knowledge of the Scottish topic, so ensure that you are confident on the four issues before the exam.

The 'Compare the views' question

This is worth 5 marks and uses two sources. The question requires a comparison of two viewpoints on an issue and a decision on whether they agree/disagree about specific points. Developed comparisons should be made to gain full marks. A developed comparison is when you identify something specific that both sources agree/disagree on and then extract the information to demonstrate this comparison from each source individually. No recalled knowledge is required for this question.

- Make an overall statement about the viewpoints of each source on the specific issue in question.

- Use evidence from each source to support your point.

- Four detailed and specific developed comparisons should be attempted in order to gain full marks.

Higher History essay – British topic and European and World topic

The essay structure for Higher History has only changed slightly, but these changes are important ones. The essay is worth 20 marks and the marks are broken up as shown below:

- Introduction **(I)** = 2 marks
- Knowledge and Understanding **(KU)** = 6 marks
- Analysis **(A)** = 6 marks
- Evaluation **(E)** = 4 marks
- Conclusion **(C)** = 2 marks

Structure

Introduction

- Start by setting the question in context. What was going on just before the event in question?
- Using the wording of the question, establish a line of argument. It is likely that a factor is mentioned in the question. Is this factor the most important in the event? Is another factor more important? Outlining this will help you with the next section.
- Outline the factors you are going to discuss to answer the question. **(I)**

Main Body

- You should start with the question/isolated factor that you will use to create your line of argument.
- Ensure you provide at least two or three pieces of evidence in each paragraph, demonstrating developed knowledge relevant to the issue in the question to support the factor and its importance. **(KU)**
- Explain how each piece of evidence helps to answer the question. After a developed point you should state how that piece of evidence helps support the importance of the factor. You can gain up to 4 marks for this.
- You can gain a further 2 marks for linking important pieces of evidence back to the question. This can also help build your line of argument. **(A)**
- Evaluation marks can come in the form of a judgement, e.g. historical importance, counter argument or historical debate. 1–2 marks are given for isolated evaluation but 3–4 evaluation marks are awarded where the candidate connects their evaluation to a line of argument established throughout the essay. **(E)**

Conclusion

- Start by answering the question and using your line of argument to do this. You should not be repeating yourself and instead you should provide a summary as to why that particular factor is the most important.

- Ensure the other factors are mentioned and that an overall judgement is made on all the factors, for example 'On the one hand … However, on the other hand … '.

Higher History topics

This book is aimed at improving Higher History source-based and essay skills. There are 20 topics to choose from for the Higher History course. In this book original source-based and essay questions have been provided for the eight most popular topics:

Scottish

- The Wars of Independence, 1249–1328

- The Treaty of Union, 1689–1740

- Migration and Empire, 1830–1939

- The Impact of the Great War, 1914–1928

There are three source-based questions for each of these topics, one each of 'Evaluate the usefulness', 'How fully' and 'Compare the views', along with complete marking instructions.

Britain

- The Making of Modern Britain, 1851–1951

There are three essay questions and one fully worked model answer for this topic, along with complete marking instructions.

European and World

- Germany, 1815–1939

- USA, 1918–1968

- Appeasement and the Road to War, to 1939

There are three essay questions and one fully worked model answer for each of these topics, along with complete marking instructions.

SECTION 1 – SCOTTISH

Part A: The Wars of Independence, 1249–1328

SECTION 1 – SCOTTISH

Part A: The Wars of Independence, 1249–1328

SECTION 1 – SCOTTISH – 20 marks

Part A: The Wars of Independence, 1249–1328

Study the sources below and attempt the questions which follow.

Source A: from the *Chronicle of John of Fordoun*, 1350.

In March 1296, the King of England, being strongly stirred up, marched in person, with a large force, on Scotland. Upon the town of Berwick, sparing neither sex nor age, the aforesaid King of England, put to the sword some 7500 souls. On 27 April, in the same year, was fought the battle of Dunbar, where Patrick of Graham and many Scottish nobles fell wounded in defeat, while a great many other knights fled to Dunbar Castle. However, up to 70 of them, including William, Earl of Ross, were betrayed by the warden of the castle and handed over to the King of England, like sheep offered to the slaughter. In this, Balliol's war, all the supporters of Bruce's party were generally considered traitors to their King and country.

Source B: from the *Chronicle of Walter of Guisborough*, around 1300.

Meanwhile two friars were sent to the army of the Scots, to William Wallace, to see if they wanted to embrace the peace which the English offered. Wallace replied, "Tell your men that we have not come for peace but are ready for the fight, to vindicate ourselves and to free our kingdom." There was not a more suitable place to put the English into the hands of the Scots. When the Scots saw that they could win, they came down from the hill. Sending men with pikes, they seized the end of the bridge so that no Englishman could cross or return. Among the English nobles cut down by the Scottish pikemen was Lord Hugh de Cressingham. The Scots hated him and cut his hide into little bits. They called him not the King "treasurer" but his "treacherer".

Source C: from Ronald McNair Scott, *Robert the Bruce, King of Scots* (1993).

Robert Bruce had no wish to prolong the war. He saw his victory, above all, as an opportunity for reconciliation and peace. Soon after Bannockburn many Scottish barons and knights who had served under the two Edwards offered to him their allegiance and were received into his peace. In November 1314 Bruce with increased confidence, convened a Parliament at Cambuskenneth. The Parliament adjudged that all Scottish landowners who had failed to offer allegiance by that date should be disinherited. His sole aim was that those who wished to regain their Scottish lands must do homage to him alone. They could no longer be feudatories in two countries and serve two kings. They must choose their nationality once and for all.

Source D: from Richard Oram, *The Kings and Queens of Scotland* (2006).

Robert was quick to capitalise on Bannockburn. Not only was he able to recover his queen and daughter from captivity in exchange for English prisoners, but this also gave him extensive resources with which to reward his supporters and subjects in order to secure their loyalty. A Parliament at Cambuskenneth was possible for Bruce due to favourable circumstances. At the Parliament in November he overcame his remaining Scottish opponents and took their lands in Scotland. Robert also intensified his attacks on northern England both in search for cash and to force Edward II to recognise Bruce's kingship of a free Scotland. By 1323 Bruce attempted to secure peace for war-weary Scotland, even negotiating a peace. Yet faced with the English King's refusal to give up Scotland, Robert had to settle for a long uneasy truce in 1323.

Attempt all of the following questions.

1. Evaluate the usefulness of **Source A** as evidence of the subjugation of Scotland by Edward I.

   In reaching a conclusion you should refer to:
   - *the origin and possible purpose of the source*
   - *the content of the source*
   - *recalled knowledge*

   6

2. How fully does **Source B** explain the reasons for the growth of William Wallace and Scottish resistance?

   Use the source and recalled knowledge.

   9

3. Compare the views of **Sources C** and **D** on the ambitions and ultimate success of Robert Bruce in maintaining Scotland's independence.

   Compare the content overall and in detail.

   5

Marking instructions

Question 1

The candidate makes a judgement on how useful **Source A** is as evidence of the subjugation of Scotland by Edward I.

Author: John of Fordoun	John was a Scottish chronicler and a secular priest who composed the majority of his work in the early 14th century. His work is nationalistic in attitude and reliable except when it came to legendary figures. This is useful as he was an eyewitness to the events surrounding the subjugation of Scotland by Edward I, but also means that he could have been guilty of exaggerating the facts.
Type of source: chronicle	This extract is part of John of Fordoun's chronicles. This is useful as he have documented events in Scotland as they happened. However, he could have embellished the facts to make them appear more exciting.
Purpose: to document the events surrounding the invasion of Scotland by Edward I	This source is possibly biased. This is less useful, especially as some historians believe Fordoun was guilty of exaggerating.
Timing: 1350	This record was made many years after the events had happened. This makes the source less useful as Fordoun's memory may not have recounted the events accurately.
Content	The King of England marched into Berwick and took 7500 Scottish lives. In April of the same year he marched into Dunbar, where many nobles fell and many fled to Dunbar castle. 70 of them (Scottish nobles), including William, Earl of Ross, were betrayed by the warden of the castle and handed over to the King of England.

Possible points of significant omission	The invasion of Edward I and the English Army into Scotland in March 1296.
	The capture of castles in Scotland by Edward I, e.g. Edinburgh and Stirling castles.
	Edward I marched north to crush John Balliol and Scottish resistance.
	King John surrendered at Montrose in July 1296 to Edward I.
	King John was stripped of his royal tunic, e.g. Toom Tabard.
	King Edward removed symbols and documents of Scotland's independence, e.g. the Stone of Destiny.
	The Ragman's Roll was signed by Scotland's nobles in recognition of Edward I as overlord.
	King John was imprisoned in the Tower of London.
	Any other relevant points.

Question 2

The candidate makes a judgement on how fully **Source B** explains the reasons for the growth of William Wallace and Scottish resistance.

Points from the source	'"Tell your men that we have not come for peace but are ready for the fight, to vindicate ourselves and to free our kingdom."'
	'There was not a more suitable place to put the English into the hands of the Scottish.'
	'When the Scots saw that they could win, they came down from the hill. Sending men with pikes, they seized the end of the bridge so that no Englishman could cross or return.'
	'Among the English nobles cut down by the Scottish pikemen there was Lord Hugh de Cressingham.'
Points from recall	Resistance to the English grew in the south-west and north-east of Scotland.
	William Wallace and Andrew Murray brought leadership to Scottish resistance and gave the Scots someone to follow if they were opposed to English rule.
	Scottish guerrilla tactics from the early days of resistance had moved towards a pitched battle at Stirling, under the combined leadership of Murray and Wallace.
	Rebellions had begun in the spring of 1297.
	The nobles Bruce and Steward had revolted against Edward at Irvine.
	Andrew Murray took castles at Inverness, Elgin and Aberdeen to show his resistance to English rule.
	Murray had also removed all English garrisons north of Dundee.
	William Wallace was present at the murder of Sir William Heselrig, the English Sheriff of Lanark.
	The Scottish victory at the Battle of Stirling Bridge, 11 September 1297.
	Scottish resistance at the battle of Falkirk in 1298 despite the Scottish defeat.

	Wallace and Murray were appointed Guardians of Scotland as a result of the win.
	Wallace invaded the north of England, around Carlisle and Newcastle, to continue his resistance against English rule in Scotland.
	Recovery of English-held castles by the Scots, e.g. Edinburgh, Stirling and Berwick.
	The changing military balance.
	Economic attempts at Scotland continuing to trade in Europe, e.g. the Lubeck letter.
	Political attempts by Wallace to gain support in Europe, e.g. France and Rome.
	Any other relevant points.

Question 3

The candidate compares the views expressed in **Sources C** and **D** on the ambitions and ultimate success of Robert Bruce in maintaining Scotland's independence.

Overall comparison:	Overall comparison:
Source C believes that Bruce did not want to prolong war and instead wanted to regain all lost land and loyalty to him as the rightful King of Scotland. He hoped to establish a new peace.	Source D believes that Bruce wanted to take advantage of the win at Bannockburn by forcing Edward II to accept him as King of Scotland. However, this took him much longer than Bruce anticipated.
Points from Source C	**Points from Source D**
Agrees – Robert Bruce had no wish to prolong the war. He saw his victory, above all, as an opportunity for reconciliation and peace.	Agrees – By 1323 Bruce attempted to secure peace for war-weary Scotland, even negotiating a peace.
Agrees – Soon after Bannockburn many Scottish barons and knights who had served under the two Edwards offered to him their allegiance and were received into his peace.	Agrees – This also gave him extensive resources with which to reward his supporters and subjects in order to secure their loyalty.
Agrees – In November 1314 Bruce, with increased confidence, convened a Parliament at Cambuskenneth.	Agrees – A Parliament at Cambuskenneth was possible for Bruce due to favourable circumstances.
Agrees – The Parliament adjudged that all Scottish landowners who had failed to offer allegiance by that date should be disinherited.	Agrees – At the Parliament in November he overcame his remaining Scottish opponents and took their lands in Scotland.

SECTION 1 – SCOTTISH

Part C: The Treaty of Union, 1689–1740

SECTION 1 – SCOTTISH

Part C: The Treaty of Union, 1689–1740

SECTION 1 – SCOTTISH – 20 marks

Part C: The Treaty of Union, 1689–1740

Study the sources below and attempt the questions which follow.

Source A: from Keith Brown, *Kingdom or Province? Scotland and the Regal Union, 1603–1715* (1992).

The last year of William's reign was overshadowed by the additional problem of the death in 1701 of Princess Anne's last surviving child, the Duke of Gloucester. As Anne was William's only heir this left the succession vulnerable, especially when Louis XIV recognised Anne's Jacobite half-brother. Consequently, the English Parliament passed the Act of Settlement, regulating the succession and making Sophia, the electress of Hanover, heir to Anne. Scottish intentions were ignored in making this decision, which was seen by the Scottish Parliament as another example of English arrogance. William's own unexpected death in March 1702 left the crown in the hands of an unhealthy, childless woman, and made a resolution of the succession urgent.

Source B: from a petition by Stirling Town Council to the Scottish Parliament on 18 November 1706.

We have considered the great affair of Union between Scotland and England as contained in the articles of the treaty. We desire true and continued peace and friendship with our neighbours in England. However, we judge it our duty to the nation and parliament, to state that this treaty will prove ruinous to our manufacturing industry, since the new freedom of trade will never balance the new insupportable burden of taxation. The treaty will deprive us, and the rest of the royal burghs in this nation, of our fundamental right of being represented in the legislative power. Thus, an ancient nation, so long and gloriously defended by patriots, will be suppressed as our dear parliament is extinguished. Scotland will be brought under a burden which we will never be able to bear, with fatal consequences which we tremble to think about.

Source C: from a pamphlet by William Seton of Pitmedden, *Scotland's Great Advantages by a Union with England*, 1706.

With Union, England secures an old and dangerous enemy to be her friend, and thereby ensures peace at home, and is safer to conduct her policy abroad. Scotland will not be alarmed by the threatenings of a powerful and rich neighbour, nor so easily put under the control of a foreign parliament. England gains a considerable addition of brave and courageous men to their fleet, armies and plantations. Scotland is now secured by their protection, and enriched by their labours. We send our produce and useful manufactured goods to them and have money and other things we need given to us. They have free access to all our seas and ports and are capable of all privileges of citizens. We are the same among them, can start colonies at a cheaper rate, and with more assurance than before.

Source D: from a speech made by William Seton of Pitmedden, on the first Article of the Treaty, 2 November 1706.

> In general, I may point out, that by this Union, we will have access to all the advantages in trade the English enjoy: we will be able, with good government, to improve our national product, for the benefit of the whole island; and we'll have our Liberty, Property and Religion, secured under the protection of one Sovereign, and one Parliament of Great Britain … let us therefore, My Lord, after all these considerations approve this Article: and when the whole Treaty shall be duly examined and ratified, I am hopeful that this Parliament will return their most dutiful thanks to Her Majesty for her royal endeavours in promoting a lasting Union between both nations.

Attempt all of the following questions.

1. How fully does **Source A** explain the worsening relations with England?   **9**

   Use the source and recalled knowledge.

2. Compare the views of **Sources B** and **C** on the arguments for and against Union with England.   **5**

   Compare the content overall and in detail.

3. Evaluate the usefulness of **Source D** as evidence of the passing of the Union by the Scottish Parliament.   **6**

   In reaching a conclusion you should refer to:
   * *the origin and possible purpose of the source*
   * *the content of the source*
   * *recalled knowledge*

Marking instructions

Question 1

The candidate makes a judgement on how fully **Source A** explains the worsening relations with England.

Points from the source	The source mentions the problems regarding the succession with regard to Queen Anne's last surviving child dying.
	The source also mentions England passing the Act of Settlement, outlining Hanoverian succession with the assumption that Scotland was included.
	The Scottish views were ignored and this angered the Scots, which was seen as further English arrogance.
	William's own unexpected death made a resolution of the succession urgent.
Points from recall	The Scots were angered by the interference of English ministers, such as Godolphin, in their affairs.
	The Scots retaliated to the Act of Settlement with the Act of Security.
	The Scots would only agree to the Hanoverian succession if they were able to issue specific conditions.
	The Act anent Peace and War meant the Scottish parliament would make all future decisions regarding Scotland's involvement in wars. This was as a result of being dragged into a war because of the Spanish Succession.
	The Wine Act meant that Scots would continue to trade with France despite the war, which angered England.
	England's Alien Act of 1705 meant that economic sanctions would be placed on Scotland. This threat would affect most merchants and the nobility.
	In April 1705, the Worcester incident – where Captain Green and two crewmen were hanged despite protests from the Queen – created even more strong anti-English feeling.
	The Massacre of Glencoe worsened relations even further.
	The failure of the Darien scheme created huge tensions between the two countries.
	Any other relevant points.

Question 2

The candidate compares the views expressed in **Sources B** and **C** on the arguments for and against Union with England.

Overall comparison:	Overall comparison:
Source B believes the Union would have a negative impact on Scotland with regard to effects on government, industry and trade.	Source C believes the Union would have a positive impact on Scotland with regard to military, industry, trade and colonies.
Points from Source B	**Points from Source C**
Agrees – Sees the importance of peace with England: 'We desire true and continued peace and friendship with our neighbours in England.'	Agrees – Sees the importance of peace with England: 'England secures an old and dangerous enemy to be her friend, and thereby ensures peace at home.'
Disagrees – Highlights the negative effects on trade: '… this treaty will prove ruinous to our manufacturing industry'.	Disagrees – Highlights the positive effects on trade: 'We send our produce and useful manufactured goods to them and have money and other things we need given to us.'
Disagrees – Sees the treaty as a negative to Scotland: '… an ancient nation, so long and gloriously defended by patriots, will be suppressed as our dear parliament is extinguished'.	Disagrees – Sees the treaty as a positive to Scotland: 'Scotland will not be alarmed by the threatenings of a powerful and rich neighbour, nor so easily put under the control of a foreign parliament'.
Disagrees – Highlights the consequences of the treaty being negative: 'Scotland will be brought under a burden which we will never be able to bear, with fatal consequences which we tremble to think about.'	Disagrees – Highlights the consequences of the treaty as being positive: 'Scotland is now secured by their protection and enriched by their labours.'

Question 3

The candidate makes a judgement on how useful **Source D** is as evidence of the passing of the Union by the Scottish Parliament.

Author: William Seton of Pitmedden	He was one of the few pro-Union Scottish voices who stood up in Parliament to speak in favour of Union. He felt Scotland was 'poor and without force to protect its commerce' and he felt that Scotland needed 'trade and protection of some powerful neighbour nation'. This is less useful as he was a minority voice in the Scottish Parliament.
Type of source: speech	The speech was made in Parliament to encourage the Scots to go for Union. This is useful as it shows us how the Scottish Parliament was still being assured of the positives of the Union close to its execution.
Purpose: to encourage support for the Union	This source is possibly biased. This is less useful, especially as some felt that Pitmedden was out for his own gain rather than Scotland's.
Timing: 2 November 1706	This speech was made just 2 months before the Treaty of Union was ratified. This is useful as it gives us a good idea of how Scotland was feeling towards Union close to the time it was ratified.
Content	The Union would improve the Scottish economy by allowing access to English trade. It would also secure Liberty, Property and Religion. The Union would lead to a united monarchy in England and Scotland.

Possible points of significant omission	The Union would resolve previous tensions such as vulnerable successions and monarchy deaths.
	There was a large amount of bribery and/or payment of arrears of salaries that encouraged some to vote for Union.
	There was a promise of compensation for the shareholders of the Company of Scotland (Darien).
	Squadrone Volante voted for union as a result of this.
	The large benefits of trade with the English colonies attracted some to vote for Union.
	Scottish peers would have access to the same privileges as the English, which included no imprisonment for debt.
	These omissions make the source less useful as it fails to show us the doubts the Scottish Government were having so close to the decision being made.
	Any other relevant points.

SECTION 1 – SCOTTISH

Part D: Migration and Empire, 1830–1939

SECTION 1 – SCOTTISH

Part D: Migration and Empire, 1830–1939

SECTION 1 – SCOTTISH – 20 marks

Part D: Migration and Empire, 1830–1939

Study the sources below and attempt the questions which follow.

Source A: from Angus Nicholson, Canada's Special Immigration Agent in the Highlands of Scotland, 1875.

> All the competing Emigration Agencies formerly reported on, are still at work as actively as ever. The New Zealand and Australian authorities are particularly alert, the streets of every town and village displaying their bills and posters offering opportunities for emigrants to gain employment and wealth. Not only so, but nearly all newspapers' advertisements are doing their full share to help. It has to be noted that a considerable number of potential recruits have been diverted from Canada to New Zealand as a result of the latter's offer of free passages. It is extremely difficult for us to attract emigrants when these territories are offering free passages while we expect the emigrants to pay their own fares to Canada. Yet land and a new life can easily be found in Canada and should not be ignored by Scottish emigrants.

Source B: from a letter by an Italian immigrant to Glasgow in 1921.

> School was a nightmare for me but my oldest brother Giacomo, a name that was quickly shortened to Jack, revelled in school life. He was a quick learner and always able to take care of himself. A few times I found myself surrounded by classmates chanting at me because I was a foreigner. Jack scattered them and they stopped bothering me completely. Our family moved house a few times in an effort to improve our life. Domenico took a job in the largely Italian trade of terrazzo tile workers and most of my brothers followed him into the trade. Meanwhile my grasp of the Glasgow dialect improved. Within a couple of years I lost all trace of my mother tongue and developed a strong, guttural Glasgow accent. In no time at all I was a complete Glaswegian.

Source C: from a report by the Immigration Agent for Victoria, Australia, 1853.

> I do not consider that the inhabitants of the islands of Scotland are well suited to the wants and needs of Australia. Their total ignorance of the English language has made it difficult for them to mix with many English people already here. Their laziness and extremely filthy habits have made it difficult for them to prosper. It would be better if such immigration was restricted at least, since these wretches have little of worth to offer this society. They have made no effective contribution to the many business opportunities to be found in Australia. Indeed, it cannot be argued other than that their arrival is having a most unwelcome and detrimental effect on the inhabitants of this colony, making little or no contribution to the economic life in this colony.

Source D: from Ian Donnachie, *Success in the "Lucky" Country* (1988).

There were many examples of Scottish achievement in Australia. Scots were early and successful pioneers in sheep farming and the wool trade, centred in places such as Melbourne and Adelaide. Scots also invested heavily in mining, at first in coal and later in copper, silver and gold. The Gold Rush of the 1850s brought to Australia a considerable number of Scottish miners, many of whom stayed after the initial gold fever died down and prospered. Shipping and trade were other areas of enterprise in which Scots excelled. Two later shipping firms were both fiercely Scottish, McIllwraith McEachan and Burns Philp. Their profits were built on the Queensland boom of the 1880s in which Scots played a large part in creating the profitable business. It should be noted that Scots made a sustained financial contribution to life in Australia.

Attempt all of the following questions.

1. Evaluate the usefulness of **Source A** as evidence of the reasons why Scots migrated.   **6**

    In reaching a conclusion you should refer to:
    *   *the origin and possible purpose of the source*
    *   *the content of the source*
    *   *recalled knowledge*

2. How fully does **Source B** describe the experience of immigrants in Scotland?   **9**

    Use the source and recalled knowledge.

3. Compare the views of **Sources C** and **D** on the contribution of Scots to the economic development of the Empire.   **5**

    Compare the content overall and in detail.

Marking instructions

Question 1

The candidate makes a judgement on how useful **Source A** is as evidence of the reasons why Scots migrated.

Author: Angus Nicholson, Canada's Special Immigration Agent in the Highlands of Scotland	He was an agent sent from Canada to find out why fewer Scottish people were immigrating into Canada. This is useful as he was an eyewitness to the methods of other countries in trying to encourage Scottish residents to emigrate.
Type of source: report	The report identified the reasons why Scots are no longer looking to relocate to Canada. This is useful as it shows how popular migrating to Canada, New Zealand and Australia was at the time, as there was such competition to encourage people to emigrate.
Purpose: to inform on the competition to attract migrant Scots	This source shows the reasons why Canada was struggling to attract emigrants.
Timing: 1875	This was during the time when thousands of Scots were migrating away from the despair and deprivation of their own country to the promise of a better life. This is useful because it gives a good idea of where people were going at the time of mass emigration.
Content	New Zealand and Australia offering 'opportunities for emigrants to gain employment and wealth'. New Zealand was offering 'free passages' to Scots. 'Land and a new life can easily be found in Canada and should not be ignored by Scottish emigrants.'

Possible points of significant omission	Overbearing landlords and lack of opportunities encouraged emigration from the Highlands of Scotland.
	Many countries would pay for the passage of the emigrants if they were good workers, particularly agricultural and urban.
	Incentives offered by foreign lands, such as free land in Canada.
	The Highland Clearances also caused Scots to leave.
	The failure of the kelp and herring industries affected migration.
	Effects of the Agricultural Revolution on farming and employment meant more Scots wanted to leave.
	Any other relevant points.

Question 2

The candidate makes a judgement on how fully **Source B** describes the experience of immigrants in Scotland.

Points from the source	'I found myself surrounded by classmates chanting at me because I was a foreigner.'
	'Our family moved house a few times in an effort to improve our life.'
	'Domenico took a job in the largely Italian trade of terrazzo tile workers and most of my brothers followed him into the trade.'
	'In no time at all I was a complete Glaswegian.'
Points from recall	**Italians:** There was a greater degree of acceptance of Italian cafes from the Temperance Movement because the cafes chose not to sell alcohol.
	Italians were accepted into Scottish society because they provided a service with cafes, etc.
	Italians kept their own identity through clubs and organisations.
	Italians suffered some hostility in the years before the outbreak of World War II as concerns grew about Mussolini's actions.
	Catholic Irish: Often resented as competition for jobs.
	Blamed for spread of diseases and poverty.
	Catholic Irish workers were often willing to work for less money than Scottish workers.
	The Education (Scotland) Act 1918 allowed Catholic schools into the state system, funded through education rates. It also gave the schools the right to give Catholic religious instruction and select their own teachers.
	The Catholic Irish had a shared experience with the Scottish workers in that they were affected by industrialisation, urbanisation, as well as fighting together during the First World War.
	Protestant Irish: Irish Protestants had a lot in common with the average Scot because of long-term and deeply embedded cultural interaction between Ulster and lowland Scotland.

Jews:

Some Jews settled in central Glasgow, typically setting up small businesses.

Anti-semitism was never that widespread, possibly owing to low numbers of Jewish immigrants in relation to other groups.

Lithuanians:

Immigrants from Lithuania were largely employed in the coal industry.

They often changed their names to integrate more easily into Scottish society.

Between the 1860s and 1914 about 7000 Lithuanians decided to settle in Scotland.

Scots complained about the Lithuanians being dirty and immoral but soon most were accepted.

At first Lithuanians were used as strike breakers but soon they joined with the local workers in taking part in the strikes.

Lithuanian immigration numbers were much lower than Irish immigrants and so not seen as a threat to the Scottish way of life by native Scots.

Any other relevant points.

Question 3

The candidate compares the views expressed in **Sources C** and **D** on the contribution of Scots to the economic development of the Empire.

Overall comparison:	**Overall comparison:**
Source C believes that all Scottish immigrants are dirty, illiterate and have nothing to offer Australia in an economic sense.	Source D believes the Scottish immigrants have created wealth for the country and have created an economic boom.
Points from Source C	**Points from Source D**
Disagrees – 'I do not consider that the inhabitants of the islands of Scotland are well suited to the wants and needs of Australia.'	Disagrees – 'There were many examples of Scottish achievement in Australia.'
Disagrees – 'Their (Scots) laziness and extremely filthy habits have made it difficult for them to prosper.'	Disagrees – '… a considerable number of Scottish miners, many of whom stayed after the initial gold fever died down and prospered'.
Disagrees – 'They (Scots) have made no effective contribution to the many business opportunities to be found in Australia.'	Disagrees – '… in which Scots played a large part in creating the profitable business'.
Disagrees – 'Indeed, it cannot be argued other than that their arrival is having a most unwelcome and detrimental effect on the inhabitants of this colony, making little or no contribution to the economic life in this colony.'	Disagrees – 'It should be noted that Scots made a sustained financial contribution to life in Australia.'

SECTION 1 – SCOTTISH

Part E: The Impact of the Great War, 1914–1928

SECTION 1 – SCOTTISH

Part E: The Impact of the Great War, 1914–1928

SECTION 1 – SCOTTISH – 20 marks

Part E: The Impact of the Great War, 1914–1928

Study the sources below and attempt the questions which follow.

Source A: from a diary entry from Private Moir of the Queen's Own Cameron Highlanders: Loos, 29 September 1915.

We were relieved on Sunday, after holding our own against the Germans' repeated counter attacks, but we were not out an hour when the lot that came in lost one of the trenches that we had taken. On Monday we had another charge and got the trench back before coming out of the trenches yesterday with about 70 or 80 of us surviving, out of the 1100 originals, "the pride of Scotland".

Sir John French came along just as we were leaving our old billets and gave us a few words of praise. He told us he was proud to meet us, and congratulated us on our fine work. He told us we had done what Camerons liked to do, and what they always did; he never knew the Camerons to fail in anything they had ever put their hands to.

Source B: from Clive H. Lee, *The Scottish Economy and the First World War* (1999).

Many of the changes caused by the war were temporary such as the readjustment of agricultural production to improve self-sufficiency and the boom in the jute industry. When normal trade was resumed in the 1920s, the massively weakened position of British manufacturers in export markets became apparent. As a consequence of the war, Scottish and British industry lost its international competitiveness. The war certainly shifted the balance of international trade against Scottish shipbuilders by increasing world-wide capacity which hit the industry after the war. Also, Scottish textile manufacturers were never able to regain the Asian markets, especially India, as the war allowed competitors to move in. But the war also demonstrated the fragility of the Scottish heavy industry base and the growing need for imported raw materials.

Source C: from W. Hamish Fraser, *Scottish Popular Politics From Radicalism to Labour* (2000).

The war years also showed that support for Scottish Home Rule had not really declined. The policy of the Scottish Trade Union Congress was to call on the Parliamentary Labour Party to support "the enactment of a Scottish Home Rule Bill". The same spirit of nationalism forced Arthur Henderson and the Labour leadership in London, much against their better judgement, to allow a separate Scottish Council of Labour with a considerable amount of self-government. At the same time, the war undermined even further the organisation of Scottish Liberalism, but also much of its moral authority. The more radical elements were disenchanted by Lloyd George's political tactics and his attitude towards strikers. Liberalism was thrown into disarray while the ILP was able to emerge as the natural successor to advanced liberal radicalism.

Source D: from T. M. Devine, *The Scottish Nation 1700–2007* (2006).

The emergence of Red Clydeside and the Labour breakthrough was only one part of the change in Scottish politics after the war. The most decisive feature was the complete collapse of Liberalism as an effective electoral force. At the end of 1916 Lloyd George had split the party and by the election of 1918 Liberalism was in disarray. Among the working classes the Labour Party was most likely to benefit from Liberal misfortunes. The Liberal government denounced strikers as unpatriotic and lost support. The ILP supported the workers' grievances over prices and rents and therefore Labour gained new support after WWI. The reward came in 1924 when Labour became the biggest party in Scotland, sending 29 MPs to parliament.

Attempt all of the following questions.

1. Evaluate the usefulness of **Source A** as evidence of the involvement of Scots on the Western Front.   6

   In reaching a conclusion you should refer to:
   - *the origin and possible purpose of the source*
   - *the content of the source*
   - *recalled knowledge*

2. How fully does **Source B** explain the economic difficulties Scotland faced after 1918?   9

   Use the source and recalled knowledge.

3. Compare the views of **Sources C** and **D** about the impact of war on political developments in Scotland.   5

   Compare the content overall and in detail.

Marking instructions

Question 1

The candidate makes a judgement on how useful **Source A** is as evidence of the involvement of Scots on the Western Front.

Author: Private Moir of the Cameron Highlanders	He was a Scottish soldier who saw first-hand the horrors of the war, specifically the Battle of Loos. He will have experienced the awful trench conditions and the high numbers of fellow soldiers lost. This is very useful because it gives us a personal account of what it was like for Scottish soldiers on the Western Front.
Type of source: diary entry	This was an entry from his diary during the Battle of Loos. This is useful as it will be an honest account written to keep a record of what was happening on a day-to-day basis.
Purpose: to record his experiences of the war	This source should not be biased. This is useful because he will not be writing it for any personal gain, as he may not have expected to survive the war, given what was happening to his fellow comrades.
Timing: 29 September 1915	This diary was written a few days after Haig's instructions to attack the Germans in Loos. This is useful because it gives us a good idea of how the soldiers were feeling after the initial attack.
Content	The soldier was relieved after surviving the German counter-attack, but concerned that their replacements had lost one of the trenches they had fought so hard to take.
	He talks of gaining the trench back again, but mentions that only 70 or 80 men survived out of 1100 originals: the pride of Scotland.
	Sir John French arrived, just as they were leaving their old billets, to heavily praise their efforts. He had explained that he had chosen to visit them because they had the reputation of never giving up.

Possible points of significant omission	The Battle of Loos saw the 'blooding' of Kitchener's New Army divisions, including Scots.
	Scottish soldiers involved in the Loos and Somme offensives suffered high casualty rates.
	Scottish units tended to be seen as 'shock' impact attack formations.
	There was controversy surrounding the role of Commander-in-Chief Sir John French, known to care about the welfare of his troops, and his failure to co-operate with the French.
	Sir John French had been replaced by Sir Douglas Haig in December 1915.
	Losses at Loos were honoured with 20,598 names on the memorial at Loos, with one-third being Scottish.
	Any other relevant points.

Question 2

The candidate makes a judgement on how fully **Source B** explains the economic difficulties Scotland faced after 1918.

Points from the source	'Many of the changes brought on by the war were temporary.'
	'The war … shifted the balance of international trade against Scottish shipbuilders.'
	The war shifted the balance against textile manufacturers, as they were never able to regain Asian markets.
	The war demonstrated how fragile the Scottish heavy industry base was and how more imported raw materials would be needed.
Points from recall	There was an initial post-war boom in some industries like shipbuilding: warship yards built passenger liners and merchant ships to replace those lost.
	The coalmines were nationalised and the miners started to make good wages.
	After the war the mines returned to their original owners.
	Lack of investment and fierce foreign competition resulted in a decline.
	The Admiralty cancelled the cost-plus system and went back to competitive tendering for orders. The demand for ships, and therefore steel, declined because of this.
	Yards suffered because of labour disputes and a shortage of material.
	Wages were cut in the autumn of 1921, men were made redundant and Yarrow's was closed.
	Industrial unrest and late delivery of ships damaged the Clyde's reputation.
	Other countries increased their steelmaking as well as their shipbuilding capacity, which led to falling demand for ships and that affected steel demand.

| | Jute prices collapsed after the war. Trade restrictions were removed. Increased competition from abroad resulted in unemployment, social misery and discontent. In Dundee, several firms went into liquidation to form Jute Industries Ltd. |

The collapse of foreign markets for herring from Germany, Poland, Czechoslovakia, Bulgaria, Russia and the Baltic greatly affected the industry.

Cheap foreign imports of food such as refrigerated meat from Argentina and frozen lamb and tinned fruit from Australia and New Zealand competed with agriculture when trade was resumed after the war.

Any other relevant points.

Question 3

The candidate compares the views expressed in **Sources C** and **D** about the impact of war on political developments in Scotland.

Overall comparison:	Overall comparison:
Source C sees the importance of the war on the creation of a self-governed Scotland and details the great negative effects on the Liberals.	Source D sees the effects the war had on popularising the Labour Party and ILP and also mentions the fall of the Liberal Party.
Points from Source C	**Points from Source D**
Agrees – Sees the effect the war had on Liberalism: 'At the same time, the war undermined even further the organisation of Scottish Liberalism.'	Agrees – Sees the effect the war had on Liberalism: '... after the war. The most decisive feature was the complete collapse of Liberalism as an effective electoral force'.
Agrees – Sees the negative effects the Liberal Party had on the strikers/radicals: 'The more radical elements were disenchanted by Lloyd George's political tactics and his attitude towards strikers.'	Agrees – Sees the negative effects the Liberal Party had on the strikers/radicals: 'The Liberal government denounced strikers as unpatriotic.'
Agrees – Sees the disorder the Liberal Party was in: 'Liberalism was thrown into disarray.'	Agrees – Sees the disorder the Liberal Party was in: '... by the election of 1918 Liberalism was in disarray.'
Agrees – Sees the ILP have a positive result from the decline of Liberalism: '... the ILP was able to emerge as the natural successor to advanced liberal radicalism'.	Agrees – Sees the ILP have a positive result from the decline of Liberalism: 'The ILP supported the workers' grievances over prices and rents and therefore Labour gained new support after WWI.'

SECTION 2 – BRITISH

Part D: The Making of Modern Britain, 1851–1951

SECTION 2 – BRITISH

Part D: The Making of Modern Britain, 1851–1951

SECTION 2 – BRITISH – 20 marks

Part D: The Making of Modern Britain, 1851–1951

Attempt one question.

1. To what extent were the Suffragettes the main reason why some women gained the vote by 1918?   **20**

2. How important were the social surveys by Booth and Rowntree in the Liberal Government's decision to introduce social reforms, 1906–1914?   **20**

3. The social reforms of the Labour Government of 1945–1951 failed to deal effectively with the needs of the people. How valid is this view?   **20**

Marking instructions

Question 1

The candidate assesses to what extent the Suffragettes were the main reason that some women gained the vote by 1918.

Introduction (2)
Sets the scene and gives the question some context: Victorian women had few legal rights. Society viewed women as wives and mothers. Women had little access to further education and careers.   **Outline other factors to be discussed:** Suffragettes, Suffragists, The Great War and changing roles of women.   **Line of argument – linked to the question.**

Knowledge and Understanding (6)
Suffragettes: Organisation built on 'deeds not words'.   Used methods such as letter bombing, arson attacks on the houses of members of government, destroyed famous paintings, chained themselves to railings outside parliament buildings.   Hunger strikes were used as political weapons, which led to changes in the law so that Suffragettes could be released before death or severe injury.   **Suffragists:**   Peaceful organisation established before Suffragettes.   Used methods such as: petitions, letters, and visits to members of the government.   **The Great War:**   Women played a great part by taking on roles such as tram drivers, farmers, working in munitions factories.   All women's suffrage groups halted to help with the war effort.   Women's contribution undoubtedly helped win the war, with 700,000 women working in factories.   **Changing role of women in British society:**   Changes in the law to improve women's rights to property and children.   Women became involved in politics after being allowed to participate in town councils.   Access to further education improved and led to women becoming involved in careers in law and medicine.   **Any other relevant factors.**

Analysis (6)

Suffragettes:

Militant methods gained publicity for the campaign.

Hunger strikes caused huge public sympathy.

The campaign led to the Liberal Government discussing votes for women; without the Suffragettes, this would not have happened.

Suffragists:

The Suffragists believed in moderate tactics to win votes.

Numbers increased to around 53,000 in 1914 because so many opposed the violent methods of the Suffragettes.

Peaceful methods gained more respect politically.

Gained support of the Labour Party to force the Liberal Government to take notice.

The Great War:

Vote seen as a thank you for all the hard work they had done.

Timing of the vote demonstrates the importance of their roles during the war.

Changing role of women in British society:

Millicent Fawcett argued that social changes were vital in winning the vote.

Women becoming respected members of society by joining political parties and becoming involved in the legal profession, which meant it was hard to avoid giving them the vote.

Evaluation (4)

Suffragettes:

Publicity of their violent methods led to the politicians branding them insane and unstable.

Not the only group fighting for enfranchisement and the differing methods and approaches weakened the impact of the different groups.

Suffragists:

Little effect and low numbers until the militant Suffragettes led many to join the more peaceful Suffragists.

The Great War:

Women who helped with the war effort were young and single. Women who gained the vote owned property and were over 30, meaning that the war effort could not have been the catalyst for the vote.

Liberal Government just wanted to avoid giving the vote to more disgruntled men returning from war to nothing. Much safer and easier to control women.

Government were terrified the Suffragette campaign would start again.

Changing roles of women in British society:
Small changes made to women's rights were a stalling method.

Suffrage seen within the context of society's changing attitudes towards women.

Conclusion (2)

Identify the most important factor in answering the question: make a judgement. Suffragettes were most important because they fell into the age bracket that was rewarded with the vote. They also terrified the government enough that the vote was easier to give than have them start up their campaign again. They were willing to push boundaries and even die for the cause.

Prioritise some or all of the other factors: the Great War was also important because women gained respect for their efforts. The Suffragists remained peaceful throughout and this gained them admiration and increased numbers. The changing role of women showed how times were changing anyway, with women achieving better vocations and improved legal rights.

Question 2

The candidate assesses the importance of the reports on poverty in Britain by Booth and Rowntree and how they could have been responsible for the Liberal Government's decision to introduce social reforms in 1906 and 1914.

Introduction (2)
Sets the scene and gives the question some context: democracy had remained unchanged in Britain; feeling that the 'laissez faire' approach was the correct one, the Liberals never felt the need for change.
Outline other factors to be discussed: Booth and Rowntree reports, national security, national efficiency and political advantage.
Line of argument – linked to the question.

Knowledge and Understanding (6)
Booth and Rowntree reports: Reports conducted by Charles Booth and Seebohm Rowntree showed that a large percentage of the public in London and York were poor due to low wages, regular sickness, unemployment and old age.
The reports proved that some poverty was beyond the control of the individual.
National security: Government were horrified when 25% of the men recruited for the Boer War were physically unfit to serve in the armed forces.
National efficiency: Concerns over Britain's ability to survive economically when countries like Germany were emerging as industry leaders.
Winston Churchill felt the unemployed had no way of finding out where the jobs were and this affected the nation's ability to stay strong economically.
Political advantage: New Liberalism was emerging and it was felt that state intervention was needed to ensure the protection of the British people for social problems over which they had no control.
'Laissez faire' Prime Minister Campbell Bannerman died in 1908, making way for the new ideas and new Liberalism.
Many working class men had the vote by 1884 and the Liberals had tended to attract many of those votes; social reform was a means of appeasing this.
Competition from the Labour party forced the Liberal party to alter their policies to gain votes.
Any other relevant factors.

Analysis (6)

Booth and Rowntree reports:

Investigations showed the government at the time how impoverished many were in Britain and how they had no control over the situation. This led to the government feeling compelled to pass reforms to improve their social problems.

The evidence provided by Booth and Rowntree gave the politicians a reason to pass reforms to help the poor, who deserved this help because their poverty was through no fault of their own.

The reports started the government thinking about social reforms.

National security:

The government realised that if they were not able to fight adequately during the Boer War then how would they protect their vast Empire from a far stronger opponent.

Reports were conducted throughout the country that identified just how unfit the nation's males were and made suggestions to the government on how to improve diet and overcrowding.

National efficiency:

Britain's industry was struggling to stay strong. Threats from other countries forced the government to rethink how to improve the health and education of the people to ensure the workforce stayed healthy, which would lead to Britain staying powerful in industry.

Political advantage:

After Bannerman died, the new Prime Minister Asquith appointed David Lloyd George and Winston Churchill to senior positions and this led to the flood of new reforms, as they were both new Liberals who believed social intervention was needed.

Evaluation (4)

Booth and Rowntree reports:

Although the reports were hailed as the main reason for the Liberals' social reforms, it is hard to ignore the other factors that had direct links to specific reforms that were passed. The Booth and Rowntree reports cannot claim to have such direct links.

National security and national efficiency:

Although the government wanted to be seen to improve their status internationally to show other countries they could protect their Empire, it is also important to note the strong link between national security and national efficiency, to help improve Britain financially and economically.

Political advantage:

Many historians feel the reforms were the result of emerging competition politically and not because of concern for the poor.

Conclusion (2)
Identify the most important factor in answering the question: make a judgement. The Booth and Rowntree reports gave the government evidence they could not ignore, which that showed large portions of the British public in poverty due to reasons outwith their control. Without these initial reports the government would have remained ignorant to the social problems affecting the people of Britain. **Prioritise some or all of the other factors:** national security and efficiency both directly led to certain reforms and demonstrated how the country wanted to remain ahead industrially and economically. Political advantage was important because the Liberals had to take account of new voters and new competition if they were to stay in power.

Question 3

The candidate assesses how effectively the policies of the Labour Government during 1945–1951 targeted the social problems of Britain at the time.

Introduction (2)
Sets the scene and gives the question some context: World War II had devastated the country and Britain needed a strong government to deal with its social problems. The Labour party targeted 'the Five Giants' outlined in the Beveridge report and looked to abolish poverty by introducing reforms and creating a welfare state. **Outline factors to be discussed:** want, disease, squalor, ignorance and idleness.

Knowledge and Understanding (6)
Want: Family Allowances Act (1945) – a weekly payment for each child. National Insurance Act (1946) – unemployment pay for 6 months and sick pay. National Insurance – Industrial Injuries Act (1946) – financial benefits for people injured at work. National Assistance Board (1948) – benefits for anybody in need. *The Times* described it as: 'the last defence against extreme poverty'. **Disease:** NHS created on 5 July 1948. Doctors, hospital, dentists, opticians, ambulances, midwives and health visitors together made up the first comprehensive, universal system of healthcare in Britain. **Squalor:** Town and Country Planning Act (1947) – set a target to build 200,000 new houses a year. New Towns Act (1946) – new towns were financed in places such as Stevenage, Basildon, Newton Aycliffe and Peterlee. Children's Act (1948) – instructed councils to provide good housing and care for all children 'deprived of a normal home life'. **Ignorance:** Education Act (1944) – Raised the school leaving age to 15. Labour introduced a two-tier secondary schooling system. School Milk Act (1946) – provided free milk to all school children under the age of 18. **Idleness:** Marshall Aid (1948) – the government used Marshall Aid (money given to Europe to help the poor) to get industry going. Labour nationalised 20% of industry including: road haulage, railways, steel and coal industries.

Analysis (6)

Want:
The three acts introduced to combat poverty meant that British people could be supported from birth, right through to death, and helped stop people slipping into poverty.

Disease:
A free medical service led to improved health across the country for poor people.

Squalor:
Between 1948 and 1951 approximately 200,000 new homes of better quality were built and this meant a better life for many people who had been impoverished before the war.

Ignorance:
The Education Act led to a clear definition of the different stages of education.

An increased school leaving age meant a more educated Britain.

Idleness:
Thousands of government jobs were created and unemployment was extremely low at around 2.5%.

Nationalisation led to a huge increase in employment and meant the government was able to create jobs.

Evaluation (4)

Want:
The National Insurance Act didn't cover everyone and you were only entitled to it if you paid in a certain amount of contributions.

Disease:
The Labour party did not realise how expensive the NHS would be and later introduced prescription fees, which meant many could no longer afford the medication.

A lot of the hospitals were not up to standard and new hospitals were not really built until the 1960s, which defeated the purpose of having a free health care system.

Squalor:
Thousands of the new houses were temporary prefabricated ones that were not built to last.

The devastation caused by the war meant that although thousands of houses were built, it was not enough to house all the people who had lost their homes. Many people in London were squatting illegally.

Ignorance:
The education system was unfair for working class children and they often didn't receive the same education as children from wealthier families.

Many felt that the eleven plus test was not fair as it decided your future at such a young age and if you failed the test you left school and were trapped in unskilled jobs that paid very little.

Idleness:

The Marshall Aid plan was a fantastic thing but it meant jobs and the economy were both heavily reliant on the money that came from America.

Thousands of women, who had proved their worth in traditionally male jobs during the war, found themselves having to go back to being wives and mothers once men returned from the war.

Conclusion (2)

Identify the most important factor in answering the question: make a judgement. It is true to say that the Labour party during 1945–1951 made some excellent progress towards targeting the social ills of people in Britain. The most important would have to be Acts that introduced insurance to cover the workers of Britain, as this meant that people wouldn't slip into poverty if they became ill or injured.

Prioritise some or all of the other factors: however, the education, housing and medical acts meant that people had a far better quality of life.

Model answer

Below you will find a model answer for Question 1 of the British section that would gain full marks and clearly exemplifies the different elements needed.

Remember:

- Introduction (I) = 2 marks
- Knowledge and Understanding (KU) = 6 marks
- Analysis (A) = 6 marks
- Evaluation (E) = 4 marks
- Conclusion (C) = 2 marks

Total = 20 marks

1. **To what extent were the Suffragettes the main reason that some women gained the vote by 1918?** **20**

It can be argued that the Suffragettes were the catalyst in gaining some women the vote in 1918. However, others factors have to be considered when looking at this question. During the 1800s the Victorian woman had very few legal rights and was seen as a wife and a mother. The Suffragettes were not the first of their kind: Suffragists, who founded the idea of women's suffrage, were the original leaders. A huge shift in the way women and their roles in society were viewed, with laws being introduced to improve their equality, was also important. (I) Many historians believe The Great War was the main reason women became enfranchised. When looking at this question it is important to recognise the importance of all the above factors and their influence on a minority of the female population gaining the vote in 1918. (I)

Emmeline Pankhurst established the Suffragettes (WSPU), an organisation built on 'deeds not words'. (KU) The militant group were determined to gain media attention for their campaign, using methods such as chaining themselves to statues inside parliament and even attempting to burn down houses that belonged to members of the government. (KU) It was these middle class women and their determination to push votes for women into the public eye that led to women over 30 who owned property gaining the vote in 1918. (A) Even after being arrested Suffragettes would go on hunger strike in prison as a form of protest; this was the group's strongest political weapon as they gained a huge amount of media sympathy, leading to more support for the campaign. (KU) It can be argued that the Suffragettes' cause pushed the Liberal Government at the time to discuss women's right to vote and without them it would not have been considered. (A) However, the publicity was not always positive and made it easier for the women to be branded as violent and insane; politicians used this argument to stop women's right to the vote. (A) Another factor that weakened the Suffragettes' cause was that they were not the only organisation fighting for women's suffrage. Although the different organisations were all looking to gain the same end result, i.e. votes for women, their differing methods and motives diluted the impact they could have had, if they had worked together. (E)

The main alternative to the Suffragettes was the Suffragists. Founded in the late 1800s the NUWSS (Suffragists) had a very different approach to gaining the vote for women: peaceful protest. (KU) Members would distribute leaflets, have meetings with members of government and ask people to sign petitions in order to gain support for the campaign. (KU) It is believed that this form of persuasion led to several members of the government accepting the idea of women's suffrage and eventually leading to women gaining the right to vote. (A) Although support for the Suffragists remained low initially, once the militant Suffragettes emerged many women joined the Suffragists as they strongly opposed the violent methods the Suffragettes used. (A) It was this increased support that led to the government accepting women's desire to be enfranchised and them gaining the vote in 1918. However, it was not until after the Great War that women gained the vote and it could have been this huge event and the role women played in it that gained them the vote. (E)

When the First World War began in 1914 women quickly became the heroines of the home front. Over 700,000 women took on roles such as tram drivers, munitions factory workers and farmers, that had to be filled while the men were away fighting. (KU) Women became a crucial part of Britain's fight to win the war and this led to them gaining respect and even changing the minds of certain government leaders like Asquith, who had previously opposed the vote for women. (A) The traditional view is that some women gained the vote in 1918 because of their effort during the war; a special thank you for all their work. (A) However, this view can easily be discredited because it was women over 30 who gained the vote in 1918 and the women who had worked in the munitions factories had been largely single, younger women under 30. (E) Another argument against the Great War being the reason for the change is that the government gave women the vote to boost their political advantage; they wanted to avoid enfranchising more men who had returned to nothing from the war, and so it would be easier to add women instead. (E) The government were also terrified of the violent Suffragettes starting up their campaign again and chose to give them the vote to avoid this. (E)

However, the vote for women was inevitable as many laws had been passed to improve women's rights and their changing role in society could have been the biggest factor in the journey towards women gaining the vote. Even the leader of the Suffragists, Millicent Fawcett, felt that changes in society were one of the leading factors in women winning the right to vote. (KU) The late 1800s saw changes like women gaining rights to their children and property, women entering further education and jobs in offices and classrooms. (KU) These changes meant that a woman had more rights and this undoubtedly led to them gaining more respect and even the vote. In the 1890s women were given the right to vote at local elections. (A) This small but important political voice led to many women becoming more involved in politics; without this initial political chance it could be argued that women might have taken longer to gain interest and desire in gaining the vote. (A) However, these laws could be seen as ways of stalling women's interest by giving them as little as possible. (A) In addition to this, if the Suffragette campaign had not demonstrated the lengths to which women were willing to go to gain the vote, it is possible that the enfranchisement of women could have taken a lot longer to achieve. (E)

In conclusion, on the one hand it is true that the Suffragettes were paramount in women over 30 gaining the vote in 1918 because the women in that group were largely in that age bracket and pushed the boundaries, showing they were willing to lose their lives to gain the right to vote. (C) On the other hand the timing of the vote being given to women clearly demonstrates the role of the war, as the law was passed in the same year the war ended. In addition to this we have the vital part the Suffragists played in starting the votes for women campaign, influencing the Suffragettes to start their own group. Finally, the role of women was changing and gave women a better and stronger place within society; without this they may not have had the confidence to start the fight for the vote. (C)

TOP TIP

Remember, you can only get a maximum of 2 marks for the introduction, 6 for knowledge and understanding, 6 for analysis, 4 for evaluation and 2 for the conclusion. This model answer shows how every point would be marked if marks were unlimited, so you can clearly see where and how marks can be gained, but in the real exam you could never receive more than the maximum for each category.

SECTION 3 – EUROPEAN AND WORLD

Part D: Germany, 1815–1939

SECTION 3 – EUROPEAN AND WORLD – 20 marks

Part D: Germany, 1815–1939

Attempt one question.

1. By 1850 political nationalism had made little progress in Germany. How valid is this view?   **20**

2. To what extent was the Weimar's economic difficulties the main reason why the Nazis achieved power in 1933?   **20**

3. To what extent were fear and terror the main reasons why the Nazis were able to stay in power during 1933–39?   **20**

Marking instructions

Question 1

The candidate assesses to what extent political nationalism in Germany had made little progress in Germany by 1850.

Introduction (2)
Sets the scene and gives the question some context: nationalism naturally grew after the defeat of Napoleon in 1815. Although the original leaders of Europe may have thought that their role and country borders were put back in place to be what they were in 1789, instead nationalism in Germany was born. However, it had failed to make any kind of progress before 1850. **Outline other factors to be discussed:** opponents of nationalism, supporters of nationalism, divisions in the Frankfurt Parliament and the failed revolution in Germany between 1848 and 1849. **Line of argument – linked to the question.**

Knowledge and Understanding (6)
Opponents to nationalism: A huge part of the Austrian Empire was German and if Germany became independent then this could cause them to rebel against Austrian rule and may even encourage others to leave. Nationalist student groups were growing and causing great concern for Metternich in 1815. The Carlsbad Decree banned student groups. The Carlsbad Decree censored newspapers. France and Russia were united in their belief that a united Germany would be an enemy, both politically and economically. **Supporters of nationalism:** Many people believed in unification to preserve German culture and identity; these people were called cultural nationalists. Some believed the unification would help the economy grow and prosper. Liberal nationalists felt that a united Germany would have a sound constitution and increased rights for civilians. The Zollverein, a customs union created in 1819, encouraged nationalism. Nationalism was encouraged by poets, historians, dramatists and philophers. Festivals encouraged the ideas of nationalism, e.g. Hambach (1832).

Divisions in the Frankfurt Parliament:

An attempt to challenge the immense political power Austria had in Germany at the time.

Failed because it had no established and clear aims.

Failed because it had no support from the armed forces.

Huge divisions between the Catholics in the south and the northern Protestants.

Failure of the German revolution in 1848 and 1849:

Workers gave up because the Frankfurt Parliament failed to prevent them from starving.

Huge reliance on Prussia, particularly their armed forces.

Disagreements over who would rule a united Germany affected support for the revolution.

Austria was still too strong and was able to crush Prussia, the strongest of the German states.

Any other factors.

Analysis (6)

Opponents to nationalism:

Many members of the separate states did not want a united Germany.

All individual states had their own ruler and did not want a united Germany because it was not clear who would rule it. They were happy to keep their own power in their own state.

Supporters of nationalism:

The Zollverein encouraged trade around the states and this led to increased national support.

The middle class and students organised events and movements to promote nationalism:
- Wartburg (1817)
- Hamburg (1832)
- Young Germany (1833)
- Rhine Movement (1840)

One of the biggest factors uniting Germany was the language.

The Grimm brothers (authors) encouraged national feeling.

The composer Beethoven encouraged nationalism.

Divisions in the Frankfurt Parliament:

Nationalists struggled to decide on the size of Germany.

Nationalists couldn't decide if the new Germany should be governed by a republic, a ruler, or both.

Failure of the revolution in 1848 and 1849:
Austria managed to get Prussia to back down in 1850 and things were returned politically to the Constitution of 1815.

Many of the state rulers objected to the actions in Frankfurt because they feared the loss of their own power.

Evaluation (4)

Opponents to nationalism:
Although the biggest effect on nationalism's growth was the involvement of Austria, the country's decline internationally would stop them affecting the unification of Germany.

Supporters of nationalism:
It does seem like the support for nationalism outweighed the opposition to it. However, the majority of the people in support of nationalism lacked the power necessary to make any changes politically and it wouldn't be until one specific state showed true power to lead the other states to unity that change could happen.

Divisions in the Frankfurt Parliament:
The Frankfurt Parliament always relied so heavily on the power of King Frederick William of Prussia and he frequently changed his mind on whether he supported the Parliament or not. However, it was clear that he only wanted to support a united Germany if he was in charge.

Failure of the revolution in Germany between 1848 and 1849:
The revolution was never going to be a success because the leaders lacked a clear idea of what they wanted to achieve.

When the rulers of the independent states granted reforms as a reaction to the revolution, they were always reforms that could be easily restored when the revolution was over.

Conclusion (2)

Identify the most important factor in answering the question: it is true to say that the opponents of nationalism affected the growth and unity of Germany before 1850. However, it is important to note that the opponents only had that amount of power because of the hold Austria had on so many of the states.

Prioritise some or all of the other factors: on the other hand, it is important to note that the support for nationalism in Germany was growing in influence. In addition to this the failure of the Frankfurt Parliament and the 1848 Revolutions meant that the growth of nationalism was mainly the result of the lack of unity in thinking and moving forward.

Question 2

The candidate assesses to what extent the Weimar's economic difficulties were the main reason why the Nazis achieved power in 1933.

Introduction (2)
Sets the scene and gives the question some context: the Kaiser was forced to abdicate after the loss of WW1. The new government would have to settle the damage the war had caused politically and socially. **Outline other factors to be discussed:** ongoing economic problems, appeal of the Nazis and Adolf Hitler, resentment towards the Treaty of Versailles and the weakness of the Weimar Republic. **Line of argument – linked to the question.**

Knowledge and Understanding (6)
Economic difficulties: Over-reliance on huge loans that were being received from the USA; any fluctuation in the economy would and did prove disastrous. Hyperinflation in 1922 and 1923 caused Germany to plunge into bankruptcy, with all citizens affected. **Appeal of the Nazis and Adolf Hitler:** The Nazi party made promises to restore German pride. They promised to give people jobs. Clever use of propaganda by Josef Goebbels. Adolf Hitler was seen as a young and charismatic leader who used modern methods to gain support. Offered very popular policies that appealed to all Germans. **Resentment towards the Treaty of Versailles:** The treaty had forced the new government to: • take full responsibility for the war • reduce their military to a state where the country was defenceless • pay reparations to cover the cost of the war • lose 10% of their land. **Weakness of the Weimar Republic:** The government started with a lack of support; it was called 'a Republic nobody wanted'. Weimar politicians were called 'peasants in a palace'. Lack of strong politicians, except for Stresemann.

Hindenburg made some foolish decisions by appointing weak Chancellors.

They underestimated Adolf Hitler.

Any other relevant factors.

Analysis (6)

Economic difficulties:
Hyperinflation harshly affected the middle classes and, as they were the natural supporters of the new Republic, they now looked to alternatives like the Nazis in their despair.

The Great Depression of 1929 forced the USA to stop the loans and forced Germany back into bankruptcy. People then looked to extremist groups for answers.

Appeal of Nazis and Adolf Hitler:
Propaganda posters showing slogans like 'Hitler – our only hope' appealed to many civilians in Germany.

Attractive policies appealed to a disillusioned voting population.

The SA were heavily used to break up opponents' meetings and gave the impression of being organised and disciplined.

Resentment towards the Treaty of Versailles:
The Germans saw the treaty as a 'diktat' and would have preferred to fight on in the war than suffer the humiliation of signing it. This common feeling led to many seeking out alternative extremist groups like the Nazis.

The treaty led to hatred and criticism; this led to the government being called 'November Criminals'.

Weakness of the Weimar Republic:
The Republic struggled to deal with any of the real problems affecting the people in Germany and this led to resentment and an increase in Nazi membership.

The German Army failed to support the Republic and this made it even weaker and subject to takeover. Revolutions and putsches proved this.

Evaluation (4)

Economic difficulties:
Arguably, even a strong and powerful government in Germany would have failed to avoid the financial ruin caused by the Great Depression. In this case, it seemed to give the Nazis an opportunity to take control.

Appeal of the Nazis and Adolf Hitler:
The Nazis were not the only group flourishing as a result of the economic problem in Germany: the Communists also saw a rise in their membership during this time.

Propaganda was used effectively by other parties.

Resentment of the Treaty of Versailles:
Although the population felt that they would have rather continue the war than accept the treaty, it is almost certain that the country would have suffered more if this had been the case.

Weakness of the Weimar Republic:
Stresemann restored faith in the Republic and brought Germany back into international favour. At this point the Nazis were seen as too extreme and largely ignored.

Conclusion (2)

Identify the most important factor in answering the question: the appeal of the Nazis and Adolf Hitler was the most influential reason for the rise of the Nazis, as their strength was what Germany needed at the time.

Prioritise some or all of the other factors: however, it is important to note that if the Great Depression that plunged Germany back into financial crises had not happened then the prosperous country Stresemann had started to build could have continued to flourish. It is also important to note that the Treaty of Versailles made the Weimar Republic weak from the start and they stood little chance of not being overthrown by the Nazis.

Question 3

The candidate assesses to what extent fear and terror were the main reasons why the Nazis were able to stay in power during 1933–39.

Introduction (2)

Sets the scene and gives the question some context: the Nazis rose to power between 1919 and 1933, taking advantage of a weak Weimar Republic. The Treaty of Versailles crippled Germany and this made it easy for the Nazis to take control as many felt they had nothing to lose. Fear and intimidation had been important in the Nazi rise to power and it would prove even more important in their maintenance of it between 1933 and 1939.

Outline other factors to be discussed: fear and intimidation, propaganda, social policies and economic policies.

Line of argument – linked to the question.

Knowledge and Understanding (6)

Fear and intimidation:
Fear of SS and SA members arresting and imprisoning people.

Use of ghettos and concentration camps to rid Germany of Jews, Jehovah's Witnesses, gypsies, homosexuals and people who opposed the Nazis.

Propaganda:
Josef Goebbels used propaganda to flood Germany with the idea that Hitler was their saviour.

Nuremburg rallies were attended.

Films were commissioned to push the Nazi ideal and to emphasize what was not considered desirable in Germany.

Economic policies:
The Nazis targeted unemployment with a good level of success, reducing it to 2.5%.

The Nazis created a scheme of public works that created thousands of jobs for Germans.

Goering's policy of 'guns before butter' meant that the country was preparing for war and had the full support of the people.

Social policies:
The Hitler Youth was created to control the children of Germany. Boys were taught to be perfect soldiers. Girls were taught to be good wifes and mothers.

The three Ks (kinder, küche, kirche) were used to control women and ensure the development of the master race. Women were rewarded for having children.

Any other relevant factors.

Analysis (6)

Fear and intimidation:

The eradication of Jews from society meant many Germans were fearful of what the Nazis would do if they were caught not following the rules. This led to the Nazis having power over the citizens of Germany and helped them keep that power.

Germans knew that if they spoke out against the Nazis they would be imprisoned or worse; this gave the Nazis the key to maintaining power in Germany.

Propaganda:

The repeated slogans meant that people started to believe that Hitler was their saviour and kept the Nazis in power.

The use of film to show how powerful the Nazis were at the Nuremburg rallies meant people were terrified to speak out against them and kept them in power.

Economic policies:

The Nazis creating jobs gave the Germans a sense of purpose and pride, which meant they wanted the Nazis to stay in control.

The country felt stronger under the control of the Nazis.

Social policies:

Creating a youth programme meant that the Nazis could have control over the nation from a very young age and children would grow up not knowing any different.

The creation of Volksgemeinschaft meant that Germans felt like they belonged and were part of something; the perks that people gained being part of the 'community' outweighed the negatives and meant the Nazis continued to keep their power.

Evaluation (4)

Fear and intimidation:

Some were not scared of the SS and SA, creating groups that opposed the Nazis and spreading the word about what the Nazis were doing. One particular group called White Rose were caught distributing flyers against the Nazis; Sophie and Hans Scholl were imprisoned and then killed for this.

Propaganda:

Propaganda only appealed to those who felt favourably towards the Nazis already. However, propaganda was also used by those who opposed the Nazis and this led to many people joining groups such as Edelweiss Pirates and Kreisau Circle to show they were against them.

Economic policies:

The Nazis hid the real unemployment figures. Jews were not counted and nor were any other groups that were placed in prison, labour or concentration camps.

If you refused to take the job allocated to you by the Nazis you were imprisoned.

Social policies:

People were fearful of speaking out against the rigid program the Hitler Youth had to follow.

Many Germans were not happy with what they had to do for the Nazis, with many SS members later talking about drinking themselves to sleep each night to avoid thinking about what they had to do.

Conclusion (2)

Identify the most important factor in answering the question: fear and intimidation were the most powerful tools for keeping the Nazis in power as they prevented the majority of the country from speaking out against the atrocities being committed on a daily basis.

Prioritise some or all of the other factors: however, it is important to mention the organisation of the country and that without the tight grip on the youth and women of the country they may not have held control for so long. Finally, the use of propaganda and economic policies lulled many Germans into believing they were living in a strong country and that their lives were better because of this.

Model answer

Below you will find a model answer for Question 3 of the Germany section that would gain full marks and clearly exemplifies the different elements needed.

Remember:

- Introduction (I) = 2 marks
- Knowledge and Understanding (KU) = 6 marks
- Analysis (A) = 6 marks
- Evaluation (E) = 4 marks
- Conclusion (C) = 2 marks

Total = 20 marks

3. **To what extent were fear and terror the main reasons why the Nazis were able to stay in power during 1933–39?**   **20**

The Nazis had a firm grip on Germany by 1933 and were determined to hold on to it. The Nazis exploited a weak Weimar Republic and reaped the benefits of a country obliterated by the Treaty of Versailles. (I) It can be argued that the use of fear and terror was an important reason why the Nazis were able to stay in power. However, this was not the only reason. The Nazis used propaganda, economic incentives and social policies to keep control of Germany. (I)

Fear and terror were key factors that allowed the Nazis to stay in power. The SS would target and eradicate sections of German society that did not fall into the Nazi ideal. (KU) Some of the main victims of this brutal expulsion were the Jewish members of society, who were persecuted and ultimately faced the concentration camps of Nazi Germany. (KU) The German people watched as Jewish people from their towns and cities became social outcasts through the boycotts of 1933 and the Nuremberg Laws of 1935. (KU) Even those who disagreed with the victimisation of the Jews did not speak through fear of being removed from society themselves: this kept the Nazis very much in power. (A) This was important because opponents to the Nazis were targeted and forced into labour or death camps. These were set up by the Nazis to create order and remove unwanted people from society. (KU) However, this did not stop all opposition; some people who opposed the Nazis set up protest groups such as the White Rose. (A) However, these groups were found by the SS and dealt with accordingly. It is argued by historians that fear and terror were clearly very important reasons for the control the Nazis had on the German people and enabled them to stay in power. (E)

The Nazis used more than just the fear of their SS and SA men. One of their other key weapons for maintaining control was propaganda. Joseph Goebbels was in charge of the propaganda machine for the Nazis and ensured that Hitler was seen as a cult leader throughout Germany. (KU) This constant bombardment of Nazi propaganda kept the Nazis firmly in power and Hitler the saviour of the German people. (A) The Nuremburg rallies were a huge propaganda event, attended by thousands; these rallies clearly demonstrated how easily the Nazis stayed in power. (KU) The Nazis would also commission films that promoted the Triumph of the Will of the Nazis. (KU) This was important because it allowed them to promote the Nazi State as powerful with a strict order to maintain control, allowing them to stay in power. (A) However, propaganda was only effective on those that were already supporting the Hitler myth. Historians today argue that the use of propaganda had only a limited impact on the Nazis staying in power. (E) It did little to convince those who did not support the Nazis. The use of fear and terror remained a far more effective tool against the enemies of the Nazis. (E)

Germany appeared economically healthy under the leadership of the Nazis and this was another reason they kept their power between 1933 and 1939. Unemployment was almost eradicated. (KU) The Nazis also created a national scheme for public works that meant the employment of thousands. (KU) These employed Germans now paid taxes that fed the economy and ultimately, the Nazis. (A) Rearmament was also a crucial factor in the continued power of the Nazis. Goering's policy of 'guns before butter' convinced a nation that 'iron makes an empire strong; butter only makes people fat' and that rearmament was a good idea. (KU) The German motorway scheme (autobahns) also led to a huge influx of jobs and a healthy injection to the economy, helping to keep the Nazis at the helm of power in Germany during the years 1933–1939. (A) However, many Jews and women were removed from employment to enable the employment statistics to appear more favoourable. (E) The creation of a successful economic policy was clearly a very important factor in helping the Nazis stay in power. Although a massive success in itself and for those who found employment, those who opposed the Nazis faced a far greater threat from the fear and terror of organisations such as the SS or Gestapo. (E)

It is important to note that the Nazis also stayed in power because of their social policies. They created an education programme for the youth of Germany based around Nazi ideals. The Hitler Youth started for boys as young as 5, who were educated towards militarism. (KU) Young girls' education would focus on becoming the perfect wives and mothers. (KU) This was important because the control put in place at such a young age ensured the growing population were indoctrinated into the Nazi way of life. (A) In addition to this women were controlled with the three Ks: kinder, kirche and kuche, meaning children, kitchen and church. (KU) Women were instructed to wear their hair a certain way and never wear make-up; this organisation of women demonstrated the great power the Nazis were able to maintain in Germany. (A) Hitler even created a national community, called the Volksgemeinschaft, convincing the Germans they had a perfect way of life. (KU) Historical debate suggests social policies were designed to brainwash the next generation of Nazis and so could only have limited impact in the 1930s. (E) Although it has been well documented that the Nazis may have felt they achieved the perfect community, this was in fact far from the truth. To stay in power during the 1930s, both 'carrot' and 'stick' policies had a vital part to play. Historical opinion now suggests that fear and terror was vital for the Nazis to stay in power between 1933 and 1939. (E)

Therefore, on the one hand it is true to say that the fear and terror used by the SS and Gestapo was crucial in keeping the Nazi grip over Germany. The prospect of being placed in a concentration camp kept thousands from speaking out against the Nazis. (C) However, it is important to note that the use of propaganda meant Germans found it impossible to escape the repeated slogans of praise for the Nazis and Hitler; messages some started to believe. Finally, the social and economic policies the Nazis used meant that Germany was controlled and organised exactly as they wanted. These powerful tools meant the Nazis had ultimate control between 1933 and 1939. (C)

TOP TIP

Remember, you can only get a maximum of 2 marks for the introduction, 6 for knowledge and understanding, 6 for analysis, 4 for evaluation and 2 for the conclusion. This model answer shows how every point would be marked if marks were unlimited, so you can clearly see where and how marks can be gained, but in the real exam you could never receive more than the maximum for each category.

SECTION 3 – EUROPEAN AND WORLD

Part G: USA, 1918–1968

SECTION 3—EUROPEAN AND WORLD

Part G: USA, 1918–1968

SECTION 3 – EUROPEAN AND WORLD – 20 marks

Part G: USA, 1918–1968

Attempt one question.

1. To what extent were divisions in the black community the main obstacle to the achievement of civil rights for black people up to 1941? **20**

2. 'The Wall Street Crash was the main reason for causing the Great Depression in the 1930s.' How valid is this view? **20**

3. Improvements in the lives of black Americans by 1968 were mainly due to changes in Federal Policy. How valid is this view? **20**

Marking instructions

Question 1

The candidate assesses to what extent divisions in the black community were the main obstacle to the achievement of civil rights for black people up to 1941.

Introduction (2)
Sets the scene and gives the question some context: black Americans had received equal civil rights and the vote when Abraham Lincoln, President of the USA, passed the Emancipation Proclamation and introduced the 15th amendment to the American constitution in 1865.
Outline other factors to be discussed: actions of the Ku Klux Klan, restrictions placed on black Americans' voting rights and strict legal obstacles to separate black and white Americans.
Line of argument – linked to the question.

Knowledge and Understanding (6)
Divisions in the black community: NAACP led by W.E.B. Du Bois was set up to be a national organisation whose aim was to gain equal civil rights legally. The group made no real progress to speak of before 1941.
The UNIA were led by Marcus Garvey who was a black separatist and believed that all black Americans should return to Africa to organise, develop and take control, making them the defenders of black people from all over the world. Many believed that fighting racism with racism defeated the purpose of trying to gain equal civil rights.
Booker T. Washington was born a slave but became an educator and believed that black Americans should accept the separation from whites and retrain and educate themselves to prove they deserve equal rights. Many black Americans felt they should automatically have equal rights because they had gained them when the Constitution was amended in 1865.
Ku Klux Klan: Racist group that would beat, torture and lynch black Americans.
Popularity soared in the 1920s.
Members included influential public figures such as police officers and court judges, making it even harder for black Americans to gain equal rights.
Many black Americans who lived in the Southern states of the USA were terrified into not campaigning for equal civil rights by the KKK.

Restricted voting rights:

Loopholes were found in the 15th Amendment that made it easy for states to introduce voting restrictions.

Black Americans who attempted to vote would be asked questions like: 'How many bubbles are in a bar of soap?' Or they were made to sit literacy tests that they had no chance of passing.

States introduced a land owning rule to prevent black Americans from using their vote.

Legal obstacles:

'Jim Crow Laws' passed in Southern states following the Civil War separated black and white Americans on transport, in restaurants, parks, toilets, etc.

Plessy vs Ferguson case led to 'separate but equal' being a nationally recognised law.

Facilities provided for black Americans were always of a lower standard.

Any other relevant factors.

Analysis (6)

Divisions in the black community:

Differing methods and aims weakened the fight for equal civil rights.

Marcus Garvey was deported after defrauding many black Americans with his cruise liner company.

NAACP's only real campaign before 1941 was in 1919 when they launched a campaign against lynching that failed to attract the support of most black Americans.

Ku Klux Klan:

Methods like burning crosses outside the homes of victims meant many were scared to speak out against unequal civil rights.

Restricted voting rights:

1898's Mississippi vs Williams case outlined the unfairness of a whole white jury in a black American's murder case. The case was rejected and actually led to more states introducing voting restrictions.

Legal obstacles:

President Wilson supported segregation by saying: 'segregation is not humiliating and is a benefit for you black gentleman'.

Evaluation (4)

Divisions in the black community:
Existence of civil rights groups proved there was a desire for equal civil rights and it would take time to gain popularity and support.

Ku Klux Klan:
Popularity of the group started to drop in the 1930s – Alabama had fewer than 6000 members at this time.

Restricted voting rights:
It is important to note that there were thousands of black Americans who were able to vote during this time period.

Legal obstacles:
The influence of the legal obstacles links well with the restrictions on voting rights and makes it a stronger candidate for being the main reason there was little progress with civil rights before 1941.

Conclusion (2)

Identify the most important factor in answering the question: make a judgement. If the early civil rights campaigns had joined together with one simple aim and method, it is possible that they would have been more successful.

Prioritise some or all of the other factors: legal obstacles and voting restrictions were the most important factors because without the support of the government at state or national level there was no way black Americans could improve their access to civil rights. Finally, the fear of the KKK prevented equal civil rights because thousands were afraid to speak out.

Question 2

The candidate evaluates the accuracy of the statement that the Wall Street Crash was the main reason for the Great Depression of the 1930s.

Introduction (2)
Sets the scene and gives the question some context: following the First World War the USA appeared to thrive and flourish, feeding the idea that the USA was the land of plenty. Herbert Hoover even boasted about the amount of cars Americans had in 1929, but 8 months later the Great Depression hit with the Wall Street Crash.
Outline other factors to be discussed: saturation of the US domestic market, weakness of the American banking system and economic boom of the 1920s.
Line of argument – linked to the question.

Knowledge and Understanding (6)
Wall Street Crash: Share prices start to collapse in October 1929 and shareholders start to sell their stocks. October 24 1929 (Black Thursday) was the first day of the crash with panicked shareholders trading in a record 13 million shares. October 29 1929 (Black Tuesday) was when 3 million shares changed hands in the first 30 minutes. Millions of people lost their savings. More than 100,000 businesses collapsed. More than 15 million people were made unemployed. **Saturation of the US domestic market:** Goods were being mass produced using new methods and this led to a saturation of the market. Huge wealth inequalities meant that there was a limited market for consumer goods and by 1929 the people who could afford those goods had already bought them, meaning that more goods were being produced than sold. **Weakness of the American banking system:** The US banking system suffered due to the lack of regulation and due to the fact that it was made up of hundreds of state-based banks. Banks would often use the savings of the American people to buy shares and make a swift profit. **Economic boom of the 1920s:** Boom was based on credit – financially, Americans were encouraged to borrow and invest in the stock market. The borrowing was based on the circumstances remaining the same and the belief that a stock market investment would lead to a large return in a short matter of time. **Any other relevant factors.**

Analysis (6)

Wall Street Crash:
The Wall Street Crash could be seen as the major catalyst for the Great Depression as it led to a loss of confidence and a complete collapse in credit.

Saturation of the US domestic market:
The lack of demand meant that it quickly became clear that the consumer industry had produced too much.

In 1927 Henry Ford stopped producing one of his cars as he realised the market was saturated.

Weakness of American banking system:
By relying so heavily on stocks and shares, the banks would be in great danger if there were ever a fluctuation in the market.

It was well known that the news of a collapsed bank would travel fast and would often lead to a 'run' on hundreds of other banks.

Economic boom of the 1920s:
Crises could have been avoided if Herbert Hoover had taken better action.

Evaluation (4)

Wall Street Crash:
The Wall Street Crash could be seen as a reaction to the problem, rather than the cause of it.

Saturation of the US domestic market:
The wealth of the country was firmly placed in the hands of the rich, who also benefitted from tax breaks. If the wealth of the country had been more evenly distributed then more Americans could have been able to purchase goods.

Weakness of American banking system:
If the banks had not been irresponsible by borrowing the savers' money it is likely that their confidence would have stayed intact, along with the money.

Economic boom of the 1920s:
The economic boom of the 1920s links well with the Wall Street Crash because if people had not been encouraged to invest in the stock market then there would not have been such an impact on the financial situation of all Americans.

Conclusion (2)

Identify the most important factor in answering the question: make a judgement. It is true to say that the Wall Street Crash was the main reason for the Great Depression in the 1930s because so many had invested in the stock market, meaning that the people controlling the money of America were not bankrupt.

Prioritise some or all of the other factors: the economic boom of the 1920s and the saturation of the US goods market were both important as it should have been clear that the credit people were borrowing would eventually run out. Finally, the unstable American banking system lacked regulation and it was difficult for people to have any real faith in a bank as they saw others collapse.

Question 3

The candidate assesses what improvements were made to the lives of black Americans by 1968 due to changes in Federal Policy.

Introduction (2)
Sets the scene and gives the question some context: black icons such as Martin Luther King had started to gain real achievements within the civil rights movement with campaigns like the Montgomery bus boycott and the sit-ins. These victories had been predominantly based in the Southern states of the USA and as the civil rights campaign moved north the campaigns would change in many ways, affecting the lives of black Americans. **Outline other factors to be discussed:** changes in Federal Policy, actions of the non-violent civil rights groups, Martin Luther King and rise of black radical movements **Line of argument – linked to the question.**

Knowledge and Understanding (6)
Changes in Federal Policy: The 1964 Civil Rights Act was a very important step in improving social conditions for black Americans. The 1965 Voting Rights Act was passed, encouraging black Americans to register to vote. The Act also abolished the literacy test. Federal court passed Acts on the unconstitutional nature of segregation in schools following the Brown vs Topeka case in 1954. In November 1956 the court ruled that segregation on buses would be ended and in 1962 the court ruled that James Meredith would be allowed to attend the University of Mississippi. **Actions of the non-violent civil rights groups:** Role of NAACP in gaining the victory in the Brown vs Topeka Case and the Montgomery Bus Boycott. Role of the SNCC in the sit-ins and how this led to desegregation in restaurants. Role of the SCLC in Birmingham, 1963 and how it led to the 1964 Civil Rights Act. **Role of Martin Luther King:** Influenced by Ghandi to campaign using non-violent direct action, which led to successful campaigns as black protestors were always seen as peaceful and brave, whereas racist individuals were seen as violent and aggressive. Martin Luther King's clever manipulation of the media helped improve popularity and success of campaigns, which led to desegregation.

Rise of black radical movement:

Black Panthers introduced social improvements for black people with free breakfasts for children, creation of the Panther Sisters and the Panther Girls.

Malcolm X was an inspirational and articulate voice for the Nation of Islam.

Any other relevant factors.

Analysis (6)

Changes in Federal Policy:

The 1964 Civil Rights Act improved social conditions for black Americans, such as desegregation, leading to better access to education and public facilities.

The 1965 Voting Rights Act improved black Americans' access to the vote. This led to more people feeling they could vote and even improve their lives because they were able to vote for people who believed in equal civil rights for black people.

The Acts that were passed led to increased confidence in the civil rights movement and led to more black and white Americans joining the cause and giving the campaigns more followers, which led to even more success.

Actions of the non-violent civil rights groups:

Victories for the NAACP led to an increase in support for the civil rights movement, which led to the lives of black Americans being improved.

The SNCC showed how the youth of America could make a difference and was the first instance of black and white protestors participating in non-violent direct action.

The SCLC, led by Martin Luther King, had many victories, especially when King allowed teenagers to participate in the Birmingham protest, which led to violence from the state police, headed by Bull Connor. The media coverage of the campaign led to increased support and more improvements through the difference made by increased solidarity and confidence in the campaigns.

Role of Martin Luther King:

King was a black icon, an articulate man who could vocalise in inspiring speeches attended by thousands, what the black population of America felt, which led to the President passing Acts to improve the lives of black people.

Rise of black radical movement:

The Black Panthers encouraged black people to be proud of their heritage and have confidence in themselves.

Malcolm X also gave black Muslim people of America a voice and an icon to follow.

Evaluation (4)

Changes in Federal Policy:
Major problems of direct and indirect discrimination remained for blacks in both the South and the North, in housing, equal opportunities, justice and employment.

58% of black southerners were still in segregated schools in 1968.

Actions of the non-violent civil rights groups:
Segregation remained in schools, with 58% of black people in the Southern states still in segregated schools in 1968.

Segregation remained in many of the Southern states like Mississippi and Alabama.

Role of Martin Luther King:
King found it increasingly hard to execute a successful campaign in the Northern states of the USA. He was assassinated in 1968.

Rise of black radical movement:
Negative media attention meant fewer Laws and Acts being passed and this had a great impact on the lives of the black people of America.

The Black Panthers' rejection of King's non-violent direct action led to an increase in militancy within their campaigns. Division within the groups led to a weakened movement.

Malcolm X was confrontational and also criticised King's methods, leading to a change in the way the media reported on the civil rights campaigns and divided the movement.

Conclusion (2)

Identify the most important factor in answering the question: make a judgement. The legal progression and Acts passed by the Federal Government are the most important factor as these were the only thing that could be policed and ensure that black people were protected.

Prioritise some or all of the other factors: however, without the civil rights groups, Martin Luther King and the black radical movement there would have been no pressure for change.

Model answer

Below you will find a model answer for Question 1 of the USA section that would gain full marks and clearly exemplifies the different elements needed.

Remember:

- Introduction (I) = 2 marks
- Knowledge and Understanding (KU) = 6 marks
- Analysis (A) = 6 marks
- Evaluation (E) = 4 marks
- Conclusion (C) = 2 marks

Total = 20 marks

1. **To what extent were divisions in the black community the main obstacle to the achievement of civil rights for black people up to 1941?**　　　　**20**

It is true to say that the civil rights groups that were established in America in the first 20 years of the 20th century were ineffective. Although black Americans had received the vote and equal rights during the Emancipation Proclamation in 1865, they were still far from equal in the years leading up to 1941. (I) However, the civil rights groups were not the only hindrance; the activities of the Ku Klux Klan, the restrictions on voting rights for black people and legal impediments all affected the progress for equal rights for black Americans before 1941. (I)

It can be argued that divisions in the black community were an obstacle to the achievement of civil rights. Before 1941 there were three popular civil rights groups fighting to improve black Americans' place in the community. W.E.B. Du Bois was the founder of the NAACP and believed it was important to fight for black people's rights using legal action, but failed to make any major progress prior to 1941. (KU) Marcus Garvey led the UNIA; he was a black separatist and encouraged black people to return to Africa, even setting up a transport system to do this, but also failed to make any sort of important impact on the civil rights movement. (KU) Finally, Booker T. Washington believed it was important that black people earn equal rights and encouraged black people to gain further education and training in order to earn the chance to have equal civil rights. This was something that many black people found hard to accept, believing they had earned that right back in 1865, when the amendment was made to the American Constitution. (KU) However, one of the main problems in gaining any success was the fact that all three groups had very different aims and methods and this made it even harder to make any progress. (E) In addition to that, Marcus Garvey was eventually deported for fraudulently stealing money when arranging for black people to return to Africa. (A) It is important to recognise that the NAACP would continue with their campaign and go on to achieve some great victories for the group. However, prior to 1941 one of their only achievements was a campaign to stop lynching that only attracted the support of white people and very wealthy black people. (A) This could have been due to fear of the KKK. However, the fact that the groups existed at all shows there were people willing to fight for equal civil rights. (A)

The Ku Klux Klan also had an important role in halting the fight for equal civil rights for black people before 1941. Although the group appeared to lose popularity in the late 1800s, by 1920 there had been an influx of new members and their terrifying methods, which included beatings, torture and lynching, prevented any black person from speaking out for their equal rights. (KU) *The KKK appeared to be more popular in the south of America, with many terrified of campaigning for equal civil rights there and this resulted in a mass migration of black people to the northern states in the 1940s.* (KU) *Easily recognisable in their white robes, the KKK would carry lit torches and often burn crosses outside the homes of their victims as a threat. This reign of terror meant that most black Americans were scared to speak out about their unequal civil rights and instead they kept very quiet to avoid the horror the KKK could inflict.* (A) *However, it is important to note that KKK membership in states like Alabama had dropped to fewer than 6000 by the 1930s and this showed the changing attitudes of Americans before 1941.* (E)

It could be argued that one of the main reasons black people made little progress towards equal civil rights is because they were prevented from using their voting rights. In the 1890s many states found 'loopholes' in the 15th amendment to the Constitution and this meant they could impose voting restrictions. (KU) *If a black person was brave enough to attempt to use their vote they would be asked questions like 'how many bubbles are in a bar of soap?' or even made to sit a humiliating literacy test.* (KU) *In the South, some states introduced a rule that you had to own land in order to be able to vote; most black people there were sharecroppers so were never able to vote to improve their civil rights.* (KU) *The voting restrictions made it impossible for black people to vote for someone who could potentially improve their situation in the community, which meant they had little chance of making any headway with equal civil rights.* (KU) *Nevertheless, some black people did manage to vote and even attempted to fight back against the restrictions that were being placed on them.* (E) *State of Mississippi vs Henry Williams is one such case where a black man appealed his murder trial because he felt the all-white jury was unfair and that the restrictions on black voters meant that there could never be a black person in that jury.* (A) *He claimed this was unfair. His case was rejected and this case actually led to more Southern states introducing restrictions on how black people could vote.* (A)

Finally, further legal restrictions were placed on black people with the introduction of the Jim Crow laws. These laws separated black and white people in schools, on transport and even in toilets. (KU) *These laws were attacked when Homer Plessy attempted to sit in a 'whites' carriage of a train. He appealed against the state decision and took his case to the Supreme Court, where 'separate but equal' (which up to this point had been a set of laws in the Southern states), was then recognised at Supreme Court level and rolled out across the country.* (KU) *These laws would make it impossible for black people to gain equal civil rights as the separated facilities they were given were always of a lower standard to the whites'. Even President Wilson agreed with the law and stated that 'segregation is not humiliating and is a benefit for you black gentleman'. With support for a law that openly segregated black people from the rest of society, there was no way that black people were going to gain better civil rights before 1941.* (A) *These laws linked in well with the restrictions on voting rights for black Americans and meant that their chances of gaining a better life were severely limited.* (E)

In conclusion, on the one hand we must not ignore the importance of the ineffective civil rights groups; if they had united as one with one aim and method it is probable that the membership of one main group would have been higher and it would have fought a stronger campaign. (C) *On* the other hand, it is more likely that the legal and voting restrictions placed on the black people of America had majorly affected their chances of improving their ability to gain equal civil rights. In addition to this, the KKK were a strong force, particularly in the south of America, with several members of courts and police forces as avid followers, and so it was always going to be difficult to speak out for your rights with the threat of a lynching not far away. (C)

> ### TOP TIP
> Remember, you can only get a maximum of 2 marks for the introduction, 6 for knowledge and understanding, 6 for analysis, 4 for evaluation and 2 for the conclusion. This model answer shows how every point would be marked if marks were unlimited, so you can clearly see where and how marks can be gained, but in the real exam you could never receive more than the maximum for each category.

SECTION 3 – EUROPEAN AND WORLD

Part H: Appeasement and the Road to War, to 1939

SECTION 3 – EUROPEAN AND WORLD – 20 marks

Part H: Appeasement and the Road to War, to 1939

Attempt one question.

1. To what extent were pacts and alliances the main methods used by Germany and Italy to pursue their foreign policies from 1933?   **20**

2. 'British foreign policy was successful in containing fascist aggression up to March 1938.' How valid is this view?   **20**

3. To what extent was the invasion of Poland the main reason for the decision to abandon the policy of appeasement and for the outbreak of war in 1939?   **20**

Marking instructions

Question 1

The candidate assesses to what extent pacts and alliances were the main methods used by Germany and Italy to pursue their foreign policies from 1933.

Introduction (2)
Sets the scene and gives the question some context: Britain adopted a policy of appeasement following World War I to avoid future conflict. They also believed Germany had been treated too harshly by the Treaty of Versailles. **Outline other factors to be discussed:** pacts and alliances, fascist diplomacy, rearmament and military threat and force **Line of argument – linked to the question.**

Knowledge and Understanding (6)
Pacts and alliances: German–Polish Non-Aggression Pact signed in January 1934 between Germany and Poland promising peace for 10 years. Rome–Berlin alliance between Germany and Italy signed in October 1936, creating a 'false' friendship between the two countries. Pact of Steel agreement between Germany and Italy in November 1939 meant they both agreed to help each other in the event of conflict. Anti-Comintern Pact between Germany and Japan, in which they agreed to support each other if they were attacked by the Communists in the Soviet Union. Nazi–Soviet Non-Aggression Pact between Germany and Russia in August 1939, giving each country time to prepare for the next step in their foreign policy aims. **Fascist diplomacy:** Germany was able to successfully weaken and destroy the terms of the Treaty of Versailles. Germany walked out of the disarmament conference after asking the other countries present to disarm. Germany left the League of Nations, claiming they were not willing to be part of it if the other countries were not serious about peace.

Rearmament:

Germany started to openly rearm and conscript in 1935 with high speed.

An emphasis was placed on the importance of having a strong Luftwaffe (air power).

Adolf Hitler had successfully conscripted over 1 million men to the army by 1939 and had 8000 aircrafts and 95 warships.

Mussolini started a rearmament programme in an effort to protect Italy from worldwide depression.

Military threat and force:

Italian invasion of Abyssinia using modern weapons and tactics.

Germany remilitarised the Rhineland, breaking the Treaty of Versailles.

Any other relevant factors.

Analysis (6)

Pacts and alliances:

By signing the German–Polish Non-Aggression Pact, Germany was able to reassure international countries that expansion was not their aim, gaining them added respect.

Rome–Berlin alliance aided the two countries' involvement in the Spanish Civil War and led to the isolation and weakness of Austria.

The Pact of Steel meant that both fascist powers were able to continue with their foreign policy aims, as they knew as a team they were stronger and less likely to be challenged.

The Nazi–Soviet Non-Aggression Pact gave Hitler the opportunity to focus on the war he was orchestrating with Europe over Poland.

This latter pact also meant that Britain lost the opportunity of an alliance with Russia, which would have weakened Germany from the eastern side.

Fascist diplomacy:

The destruction of the Treaty of Versailles meant that Hitler was able to achieve his military and foreign policy aims.

Hitler was able to achieve these aims using diplomatic and 'peaceful' intentions as well as 'reasonable' demands, especially as Britain was sympathetic towards Germany and felt they were too harshly punished with the Treaty of Versailles.

Hitler was able to rearm, start conscription and remilitarise the Rhineland after declaring the other countries were not following their own plans to demilitarise. Obviously Germany had been forced to demilitarise, so this was not a hard thing for Germany to demand.

Rearmament:

Germany's ground, air and sea power by 1939 was such that they were able to successfully invade Poland, knowing they were an equal match for the allies if they chose to retaliate.

Italy's modern navy was a serious threat to Britain and their dominance of the Mediterranean.

Military threat and force:

Italy was able to invade Abyssinia because Britain was so fearful of provoking Mussolini into the Mediterranean where they had large naval bases.

Hitler gambled and marched his troops into the Rhineland with no reaction from Britain or France.

Evaluation (4)

Pacts and alliances:

Germany and Italy entered into these alliances and agreements knowing that when the time came they would have to 'double-cross' the other when it came to fully executing their aims.

If Hitler had not agreed to the Nazi–Soviet Non-Aggression Pact it is likely that he would not have been able to progress with his expansion aims, due to threats from the eastern border.

Fascist diplomacy:

The 'reasonable' term Hitler demanded at the Disarmament Conference led to him being able to rearm his country; this links perfectly by showing the importance of rearmament for Germany in achieving their aims.

Rearmament:

Rearmament links well with pacts and alliances as a factor because the fascist powers used these alliances for safety and they ensured no threat while armies were being built up.

Military threat and force:

Even though Britain backed out of the Hoare–Laval Pact after a British public outcry at the aggression against the innocent Abyssinians, Italy continued to conquer the area and achieved their plan. This links well with the pacts and alliances factor as it points out how the military threat of force was more important in this instance.

Conclusion (2)

Identify the most important factor in answering the question: make a judgement. On the one hand it is true to say that the plethora of pacts and alliances that the fascist countries participated in were crucial in achieving their aims, as without the protection and promises of other countries they would not have been so successful.

Prioritise some or all of the other factors: on the other hand, the speed of rearmament, fascist diplomacy and military threat of force from these countries also heavily contributed, especially as it was at a time when Britain and France were still reeling after World War I socially, economically and militarily.

Question 2

The candidate assesses whether the view that British foreign policy was successful in containing fascist aggression up to March 1938 is valid.

Introduction (2)
Sets the scene and gives the question some context: Britain adopted a policy of appeasement following World War I to avoid future conflict. They also believed Germany had been treated too harshly by the Treaty of Versailles.
Outline other factors to be discussed: Abyssinia, Rhineland, Anglo–German Naval Pact and Anschluss.
Line of argument – linked to the question.

Knowledge and Understanding (6)
Abyssinia:
Abyssinia was invaded by Italy using poison gas and Britain did not use force to stop the increasing powers and aggression of the fascist country.
Mussolini revealed plans for a new Roman Empire in the Adriatic, the Mediterranean and North Africa.
Rhineland:
Adolf Hitler attended the disarmament conference held by the League of Nations and demanded that the countries disarm.
Hitler used their refusal to his advantage and announced he would rearm and remilitarise the Rhineland.
Britain refused to intervene and simply said that the Germans were going into their own back yard.
Anglo–German Naval Pact:
Britain agreed to let Germany have a navy at 35% of the size of the British Navy.
The Anglo–German Naval Agreement of 1935 saw Hitler and Chamberlain working together. Chamberlain saw this as a positive because he felt he had the fascist leader under control with this agreement. It did mean that Britain was breaking the very treaty they had helped create after the First World War to keep Germany weak. However, the growth of the Luftwaffe continued to concern Britain and several historians feel this Pact was a failure for British foreign policy because it allowed Germany to rearm and introduce conscription with Britain's permission.
Anschluss:
Germany achieved Anschluss (unification of Germany and Austria) without a reaction from Britain.
Any other relevant factors.

Analysis (6)

Abyssinia:

Initial victory for British foreign policy when Britain and France successfully united with Italy in the Stresa Front in 1935.

Invasion of Abyssinia was a failure for British foreign policy because they failed to intervene.

Helped Italy conquer Abyssinia by creating the Hoare–Laval Pact, which was another blow for British foreign policy because it showed they were willing to negotiate with fascist countries.

Rhineland:

The British Government felt that Germany had been treated far too harshly with the Treaty of Versailles and allowed Germany to rearm and remilitarise the Rhineland.

At this point the British public were happy with this because many were still feeling the effects of the First World War; after losing so many of their men, the women of the country were not willing to go to war again.

Britain was restricted in its military capacity and would not have been able to fight Germany at this point had a war been started.

Anglo–German Naval Pact:

Chamberlain saw this as a positive because he believed he had the fascist leader under control with this agreement.

Anschluss:

Britain believed the large population of Austria had wanted Anschluss.

No conflict occurred in Austria when it happened; leading Britain to think the Austrians wanted Anschluss.

Evaluation (4)

Abyssinia:

There was a backlash from the British public when the plans for the Hoare–Laval Pact were leaked, making appeasement a less successful policy for Britain.

Rhineland:

Many historians feel this was a bad policy because it gave fascist Germany the opportunity to grow stronger.

At this point Germany would have been far too weak to fight back and may have halted all fascist progress in Germany if Britain had demonstrated power and refused to let Germany break the treaty.

Anglo–German Naval Pact:

Britain was breaking the Treaty of Versailles, which had been designed to keep Germany weak after the destruction of World War I.

The growth of the Luftwaffe concerned Britain and several historians feel this Pact was a failure for British foreign policy because it allowed Germany to rearm and introduce conscription.

Anschluss:

Another revision of the Treaty of Versailles that Britain had helped create.

Winston Churchill warned the Prime Minister against letting Hitler gain more power as he knew that it would only be a matter of time before Hitler's expansionist foreign policy would affect Britain directly.

Conclusion (2)

Identify the most important factor in answering the question: make a judgement. On the one hand appeasement can be seen as a useful tool that slowed the expansionist actions of the fascist powers, giving Britain valuable time to rearm after World War I and giving the public a chance to get mentally, physically and militarily ready for another total war.

Prioritise some or all of the other factors: on the other hand, if Britain had reacted quicker to fascist aggression and responded at the early stages then it is possible that World War II could have been avoided because Germany would not have been able to build up their military to compete with Britain.

Question 3

The candidate assesses to what extent the invasion of Poland was the main reason for the decision to abandon the policy of appeasement and declare war in 1939.

Introduction (2)
Sets the scene and gives the question some context: Britain adopted a policy of appeasement following World War I to avoid future conflict. They also believed that the country needed time to recover socially, economically and militarily.
Outline other factors to be discussed: British abandonment of the policy of appeasement, importance of the Nazi–Soviet Pact, British diplomacy and relations with the Soviet Union, the occupation of Bohemia and the collapse of Czechoslovakia.
Line of argument – linked to the question.

Knowledge and Understanding (6)
British abandonment of the policy of appeasement: The invasion of Bohemia and Moravia in Czechoslovakia increased the growing concerns Britain had over Germany.
Germany annexed the province of Memel in Lithuania and this further convinced Britain of Germany's threat to south-eastern Europe.
Chamberlain made a promise of a declaration of war if Poland was invaded, abandoning the policy of appeasement.
Importance of the Nazi–Soviet Pact: In August 1939 Germany and the Soviet Union made the shock decision to sign the Nazi–Soviet Pact, promising not to go to war with each other and to invade and divide Poland up between the two countries.
This pact gave Germany the freedom to focus their attention on the western side of their country as they had assurances from the Soviet Union.
British diplomacy and relations with the Soviet Union: The British Foreign Secretary, Lord Halifax had been invited to Russia by Stalin to discuss an alliance against Germany, but he refused to go as Britain feared Russian Communism and saw their army as too weak to be a good opposition to Hitler and Germany.
Britain sent a military mission to discuss an alliance but travel issues meant they did not arrive in Leningrad for five days.
Occupation of Bohemia and Moravia: After Hitler broke the Munich Agreement and invaded Czechoslovakia in March 1939, Chamberlain knew Hitler would not stop his expansion plans.
Britain realised that Hitler was not just interested in ex-German territories and instead was looking to expand further into Europe.
Any other relevant factors.

Analysis (6)

British abandonment of the policy of appeasement:

After promising to leave German expansion at the Sudetenland during the Munich Agreement, Hitler had destroyed any hope Chamberlain had for peace by invading the remainder of Czechoslovakia and it was at this point that Britain knew they would probably have to go to war.

Nevertheless, the British public and press appeared to be indifferent about the invasion of Czechoslovakia until the middle of 1938. However, they did start to react and objected to a small country being bullied, leading Chamberlain to change his initial lukewarm reaction to the abandonment of appeasement, if Germany invaded Poland.

Importance of the Nazi–Soviet Pact:

This pact put an end to the on-going talks between Britain, France and the Soviet Union and the guarantees that were being made to Poland.

Hitler genuinely believed that Britain and France would not react to his 'Lebensraum' foreign policy aims and would instead continue with their belief in appeasement.

British diplomacy and relations with the Soviet Union:

Stalin was already suspicious over Britain's reasons for negotiation talks and these suspicions grew when Britain refused to let Russia react if Hitler was to send troops into Poland. Britain had already given in to Hitler several times and Stalin felt they would be sure to do it again over Russia. The breakdown in communication led to Stalin opening talks with Hitler, which led to war.

Occupation of Bohemia and Moravia:

Prime Minister Neville Chamberlain felt betrayed by Adolf Hitler and had truly believed he'd secured peace with the Munich Agreement.

The British public also understood that Germany was not going to stop and that the country would be pulled into war, it was just a matter of time.

Evaluation (4)

British abandonment of the policy of appeasement:

However, even at this point Chamberlain continued with appeasement and gave Germany one last chance to stop their expansion. He proclaimed that only if Hitler invaded Poland would Britain declare war.

Importance of the Nazi–Soviet Pact:

Britain found the pact hard to believe, as it was well known that Hitler and Stalin hated each other. This further secured Britain's belief that the pact was simply a ploy to kill time and prepare militarily and economically for inevitable war. This factor links well with British diplomacy and relations with the Soviet Union as it shows that Russia was becoming more aware that it would be in Germany's plans to attack their country and they had to be selfish and give themselves time to prepare for that. It also showed Britain that the Soviet Union knew this and made the outbreak of war more predictable.

British diplomacy and relations with the Soviet Union:
The communication difficulties between Britain and Russia ultimately led to the alliance of Hitler and Stalin, linking well to the Nazi–Soviet Pact that both leaders signed to secure their countries before preparing for war.

Occupation of Bohemia and Moravia:
Chamberlain realised that the policy of appeasement would not work on Hitler and this links well with the abandonment of appeasement leading to the declaration of war.

Conclusion (2)

Identify the most important factor in answering the question: make a judgement. On the one hand it is true to say that the British abandonment of appeasement led to World War II, as it was at this point that Britain realised it would have to take a hard line with Germany to stop their expansion plans.

Prioritise some or all of the other factors: on the other hand, if Britain had avoided the Nazi–Soviet Pact by entering into talks with Russia earlier it is possible war could have been delayed or even prevented. However, it has to be noted that Germany's Lebensraum aims were unrelenting and Hitler would not have stopped until war was declared to stop him.

Model answer

Below you will find a model answer for Question 2 of the Appeasement section that would gain full marks and clearly exemplifies the different elements needed.

Remember:

- Introduction (I) = 2 marks
- Knowledge and Understanding (KU) = 6 marks
- Analysis (A) = 6 marks
- Evaluation (E) = 4 marks
- Conclusion (C) = 2 marks

Total = 20 marks

2. **'British foreign policy was successful in containing fascist aggression up to March 1938.' How valid is this view?**   20

Britain's foreign policy had some success at containing fascist aggression up to March 1938. Fascist foreign policy rapidly progressed after 1933 and Britain's instant reaction was the policy of appeasement, a policy they had adopted following the First World War, believing it would prevent future conflicts and preserve peace. Britain genuinely thought Germany had been treated unfairly after the war and that when they started to demand the reverse of some of the Treaty of Versailles terms, Britain felt this was understandable. (I) However, certain events in the run up to March 1938 would test the achievements of appeasement. These events were crucial factors in identifying the true success of appeasement: Abyssinia, Rhineland, the Naval Agreement and the Anschluss. (I)

When Abyssinia was invaded by Italy many believed it was a sign of how Britain was not willing to use force to stop the increasing power and aggression of fascist powers. This is particularly true when Mussolini's plans for a new Roman Empire in the Adriatic, the Mediterranean and North Africa were revealed. (KU) Italy's aggressive invasion of Abyssinia using poison gas was a great blow for British foreign policy because they had hoped to make an ally of Italy. (KU) Britain failed to intervene in the Abyssinia affair, especially as they had initially been hopeful of gaining Italy as an ally when the two countries, joined by France, had agreed to unite against Hitler and Germany, creating the Stresa Front in 1935. (A) This was an example of when the appeasement policy appeared to be working for Britain. (A) However, this was short lived; the Hoare–Laval Pact, an agreement between France and Britain to give Italy to Abyssinia, was leaked and created tension for the League of Nations. (A) The League did nothing and by 1936 Italy had conquered Abyssinia. In fact, this pact led to a huge British public backlash, as they felt betrayed by a government who would agree to support Italy's fascist aggression. (E)

When Adolf Hitler attended the disarmament conference held by the League of Nations and demanded that the countries in attendance disarm, it was quickly apparent how he would use this event to his advantage. (KU) After the other nations refused, Hitler despaired and announced he would rearm and remilitarise the Rhineland. (KU) It was at this point that Britain failed to act and instead followed a policy that felt sympathy for Germany after their treatment with the Treaty of Versailles. (KU) By letting Hitler remilitarise the Rhineland, they had allowed him to secure his western frontier against French attack and this meant he could now turn his attention towards the eastern frontier. At this time Britain was still reeling from the First World War and in that sense the British Government acted in the public's interest to appease Hitler. (A) *If they had refused to let Germany rearm and remilitarise, then there could have been dire consequences for Britain; something for which they were not militarily or socially ready. (A) However, it is also important to mention that if Britain had exercised a stronger foreign policy at this time, Germany would have instantly backed down, as the country was not powerful enough due to the terms of the Versailles treaty. (E)*

When Britain agreed to let Germany rearm their Navy at 35% of the size of Britain's this could be seen as a victory for Britain. This was the Anglo–German Naval Agreement of 1935 and saw Hitler and Chamberlain working together. (KU) Chamberlain saw this as a positive because he felt he had the fascist leader under control with this agreement. It did mean that Britain was breaking the very treaty they had helped create after the First World War to keep Germany weak. (KU) However, the growth of the Luftwaffe continued to concern Britain and several historians feel this Pact was a failure for British foreign policy because it allowed Germany to rearm and introduce conscription with Britain's permission. (E)

Finally, when Germany annexed Austria during Anschluss it was done without a reaction from Britain. (KU) Britain had believed that it was something the large population of Austria had wanted, especially when no conflict took place in the country at the time it happened. (A) Although it was yet another revision of the Treaty of Versailles, the British Government felt it was not of concern to them, but Winston Churchill warned the Prime Minister against letting Hitler gain more power as he knew that it would only be a matter of time before Hitler's expansionist foreign policy would affect Britain directly. (E)

In conclusion, on the one hand Britain was wise to adopt the policy of appeasement as it gave the country time to prepare for another war both militarily and socially. (C) On the other hand, if Hitler had been prevented from remilitarising the Rhineland and Mussolini had been stopped before occupying Abyssinia, then they would not have gained the power necessary to occupy other countries so aggressively. (C)

TOP TIP

Remember, you can only get a maximum of 2 marks for the introduction, 6 for knowledge and understanding, 6 for analysis, 4 for evaluation and 2 for the conclusion. This model answer shows how every point would be marked if marks were unlimited, so you can clearly see where and how marks can be gained, but in the real exam you could never receive more than the maximum for each category.